Bridging Learning In and Out of the Classroom

edited by Mervyn Skuy
and Mandia Mentis
in collaboration with Reuven Feuerstein

Cognitive Research Program
Division of Specialized Education
University of the Witwatersrand
South Africa

Manual Series
Cognitive Research Program
Division of Specialized Education
University of the Witwatersrand
Director: Professor Mervyn Skuy

Cognitive Research Program Manual Team:
Editor: Mervyn Skuy
Coordinator: Mandia Mentis
Marilyn Dunn
Fleur Durbach
Marténe Mentis

Acknowledgments:
Financial assistance in producing this series is gratefully acknowledged from:
Center for Science Development, Human Sciences Research Council
SmithKline Beecham
Beckman Instruments (Pty) Ltd.
University of the Witwatersrand Senate Research Committee

Bridging Learning In and Out of the Classroom

Publishing by SkyLight Training and Publishing Inc.
2626 S. Clearbrook Dr., Arlington Heights, IL 60005
800-348-4474 or 847-290-6600
Fax 847-290-6609
info@iriskylight.com
http://www.iriskylight.com

Senior Vice President, Product Development: Robin Fogarty
Manager, Product Development: Ela Aktay
Acquisitions Editor: Jean Ward
Editor: Sue Schumer
Cover Designer: David Stockman
Illustrators: David Stockman and Kristen Christensen
Book Designer: Bruce Leckie
Formatter: Donna Ramirez
Production Supervisor: Bob Crump
Proofreader: Martha White
Indexer: Schroeder Indexing

© 1999 SkyLight Training and Publishing Inc.
All rights reserved.
Printed in the United States of America

LCCCN: 98-61160
ISBN 1-57517-114-7

2160B-V
Item Number 1679

ZYXWVUTSRQPONMLKJIHGFEDCB
06 05 04 03 02   15 14 13 12 11 10 9 8 7 6 5 4 3 2

Preface

Bridging Learning In and Out of the Classroom is aimed at providing illustrations and applications of Reuven Feuerstein's Instrumental Enrichment (IE) approach. His theory is part of contemporary developments in cognitive psychology, which have culminated in the burgeoning field of cognitive education, a field that represents an antidote to the current sterility and ineffectiveness of many education systems.

Cognitive education refers to the development of thinking skills, the enhancement of adaptive behavior, and the promotion of effective functioning and self-realization. The underlying philosophy of cognitive education, which stresses individual and social modifiability, awareness, and the education of intellectual and other processes, has particular relevance for today's multicultural society.

The cognitive approach to intercultural rapprochement, understanding, coexistence, and integration recognizes that the reconciling of previously disparate and conflictual elements of a population into a tapestry of blending elements requires more than goodwill, or interpersonal contact. Rather, in line with the approach of cognitive education to human functioning generally, there is a recognition of the role that must be played by such dimensions of human functioning as understanding, knowledge, awareness, and the ability to process and regulate information.

The development of contemporary theories of intelligence and thinking has been associated with concomitant developments in technologies or approaches to implement these theoretical developments. In other words, recognition that cognitive development in general and thinking skills in particular should be central to the educational process and goals has been accompanied by the development of various programs to enhance thinking.

Feuerstein's IE program is a prototype of such programs, and is arguably the most advanced and multifaceted of these approaches. It is developed systematically from theory; it captures the various elements of cognitive education postulated above; it provides a springboard for a holistic cognitive-effective approach to education; and it is particularly amenable to cross-cultural and intercultural applications.

An attempt is made in this resource to illustrate and exemplify the multifaceted applicability of Instrumental Enrichment (IE) by giving examples of activities that teach the various cognitive operations contained in the IE program. Not only do these illustrations of the applications of IE provide a basis for actual activities, but they also demonstrate that IE has relevance for thinking in relation to the conventional school curriculum, as well as the development of thinking skills in nonformal and informal educational settings. The richness of IE in promoting creative thinking and in dealing with emotional development and its cross-cultural relevance, are also exemplified. Thus, these activities provide an illustration of what creative readers can develop for themselves.

Most important, this book is not intended as a substitute for the IE program, but as a companion volume to it. It is important that a systematic and comprehensive approach is taken to implementing the IE program, the ease of which is aided by *Bridging Learning In and Out of the Classroom*.

Apart from the activities suggested in this book, mention is made in each of the fourteen chapters of the relevance and importance of the particular cognitive operation under review, and a range of applications of that operation is enumerated. This has been done in order to ensure that the "meaning" and the "transcendence" of each cognitive operation is mediated. This represents the implementation of two of Feuerstein's criteria of mediated learning, without which a cognitive operation cannot be taught effectively. Thus, we are modeling here what should form part of any activity initiated by a teacher/parent/counselor to enhance a cognitive operation in a child—namely, the mediation of its meaning and its generalizability. Indeed, mediation is the central underlying construct of theory, and is the essential mechanism for promoting cognition and learning.

Another aspect of Feuerstein's theory covers the cognitive functions that are the prerequisites for developing and using cognitive operations. The application of these cognitive functions is exemplified in each of the chapters in this book.

Bridging Learning In and Out of the Classroom has been brainstormed by a group process, and forms a product of the Cognitive Research Program (CRP). See pages 123–124 for information on the manual team who developed this resource at the University of the Witwatersrand in South Africa, including information on Reuven Feuerstein. *Mediated Learning In and Out of the Classroom,* also published by SkyLight Training and Publishing Inc., is another useful resource that complements the IE program, also developed by the Cognitive Research Program.

What It's All About
- a practical resource designed to
  → outline the thinking skills of Feuerstein's Instrumental Enrichment (IE) Program
  → bridge the IE thinking skills to the following areas:
    - the school
    - the home
    - the community

Bridging Learning In and Out of the Classroom

Who Can Use It?
→ educators
→ parents and caregivers
→ counselors
→ therapists
→ community workers

Why Could You Use It?
→ to encourage metacognition ("thinking about thinking") in home, school, and community settings
→ to promote bridging of thinking skills taught in the IE program

Contents

Introduction ix

Chapter 1: Organization of Dots 1
What Is Organization? 2
Why Is Organization Important? 2
When and Where Do We Organize? 2
Bridging—In the School 3
Bridging—In the Home 4
Bridging—In the Community 5
Work Pages 7

Chapter 2: Comparisons 9
What Are Comparisons? 10
Why Are Comparisons Important? 10
When and Where Do We Compare? 10
Bridging—In the School 11
Bridging—In the Home 12
Bridging—In the Community 13
Work Pages 15

Chapter 3: Orientation in Space I 17
What Is Orientation in Space I? 18
Why Is Orientation in Space I Important? 18
When and Where Do We Use Orientation in Space I? 18
Bridging—In the School 19
Bridging—In the Home 20
Bridging—In the Community 21
Work Pages 23

Chapter 4: Analytic Perception 25
What Are Analysis and Synthesis? 26
Why Are Analysis and Synthesis Important? 26
When and Where Do We Analyze and Synthesize? 26
Bridging—In the School 27
Bridging—In the Home 28
Bridging—In the Community 29
Work Pages 31

Chapter 5: Categorization 33
What Is Categorization? 34
Why Is Categorization Important? 34
When and Where Do We Categorize? 34
Bridging—In the School 35
Bridging—In the Home 36
Bridging—In the Community 37
Work Pages 39

Chapter 6: Illustrations 41
  What Is Problem Solving? 42
  Why Is Problem Solving Important? 42
  When and Where Do We Use Problem Solving? 42
  Bridging—In the School 43
  Bridging—In the Home 44
  Bridging—In the Community 45
  Work Pages 47

Chapter 7: Family Relations 49
  What Are Family Relations? 50
  Why Are Family Relations Important? 50
  When and Where Do We Need to Describe Family Relations? 50
  Bridging—In the School 51
  Bridging—In the Home 52
  Bridging—In the Community 53
  Work Pages 55

Chapter 8: Temporal Relations 57
  What Are Temporal Relations? 58
  Why Are Temporal Relations Important? 58
  When and Where Do We Use Temporal Relations? 58
  Bridging—In the School 59
  Bridging—In the Home 60
  Bridging—In the Community 61
  Work Pages 63

Chapter 9: Orientation in Space II 65
  What Is Orientation in Space II? 66
  Why Is Orientation in Space II Important? 66
  When and Where Do We Use Orientation in Space II? 66
  Bridging—In the School 67
  Bridging—In the Home 68
  Bridging—In the Community 69
  Work Pages 71

Chapter 10: Instructions 73
  What Are Instructions? 74
  Why Are Instructions Important? 74
  When and Where Do We Use Instructions? 74
  Bridging—In the School 75
  Bridging—In the Home 76
  Bridging—In the Community 77
  Work Pages 79

Chapter 11: Numerical Progressions 81
  What Are Numerical Progressions? 82
  Why Are Numerical Progressions Important? 82
  When and Where Do We Use Numerical Progressions? 82
  Bridging—In the School 83
  Bridging—In the Home 84
  Bridging—In the Community 85
  Work Pages 87

Chapter 12: Transitive Relations 89
- What Are Transitive Relations? 90
- Why Are Transitive Relations Important? 90
- When and Where Do We Use Transitive Relations? 90
- Bridging—In the School 91
- Bridging—In the Home 92
- Bridging—In the Community 93
- Work Pages 95

Chapter 13: Syllogisms 97
- What Are Syllogisms? 98
- Why Are Syllogisms Important? 98
- When and Where Do We Use Syllogisms? 98
- Bridging—In the School 99
- Bridging—In the Home 100
- Bridging—In the Community 101
- Work Pages 103

Chapter 14: Representational Stencil Design 105
- What Is Representational Stencil Design (RSD)? 106
- Why Is RSD Important? 106
- When and Where Do We Use RSD? 106
- Bridging—In the School 107
- Bridging—In the Home 108
- Bridging—In the Community 109
- Work Pages 113

Appendix 1: Answers to Work Pages (True/False Questions) 117

Appendix 2: 10 Criteria of Mediated Learning Experience (MLE) 118

Appendix 3: Lists of Cognitive Functions and Dysfunctions 119

About the Cognitive Research Program Manual Team 123

Bibliography 125

Index 127

Introduction

Putting Feuerstein's Program Into Practice

What are the building blocks of efficient thinking? How can teachers use subject teaching to promote cognitive development? How can parents or caretakers teach children thinking skills within the home? How can thinking skills promote interpersonal and affective development, enhance creativity, and facilitate multicultural awareness?

This book attempts to answer these questions by bridging thinking skills from fourteen instruments of Feuerstein's Instrumental Enrichment (IE) program to the areas of school, home, and community.

Who Is Feuerstein and What Is IE?

Reuven Feuerstein is an internationally renowned Israeli professor of psychology and a scholar in the field of child development. Through his work with low functioning and disadvantaged individuals, he developed innovative methods of testing and teaching. In common with other contemporary psychologists, he rejects that static belief that people are born with a certain intelligence that remains fixed throughout life. In contrast, he shows that people have the potential to change and are modifiable if provided with the right of kind of interaction.

The "right kind of interaction" he calls mediated learning. Through mediated learning, the individual develops efficient thinking skills that enable him or her to become an autonomous and independent learner. The cognitive functions are the prerequisites or building blocks of effective learning.

The cognitive functions and dysfunctions listed in Appendix 3 of this book are helpful in identifying and understanding the reasons for an individual's failure on or poor performance of a task. Once the deficient functions have been identified, the individual may be helped by correcting and redeveloping these cognitive functions through providing appropriate and sufficient mediation. Feuerstein has developed a thinking skills program called Instrumental Enrichment (IE) which aims at remediating the cognitive dysfunctions.

Feuerstein's IE program makes use of pencil-and-paper exercises to develop thinking skills. The IE program consists of fourteen instruments that introduce fourteen different thinking skills or cognitive operations. In this book, these thinking skills are described and then bridged (applied) to the areas of school, home, and community.

> *"Instrumental Enrichment is most simply described as a strategy for learning to learn. It uses abstract, content-free, organizational, spatial, temporal and perceptual exercises that involve a wide range of mental operations and thought processes. The aim of the Feuerstein Instrumental Enrichment (FIE) program is to change the overall cognitive structure of the (impaired) performer by transforming his passive and dependent cognitive style into that characteristic of an autonomous and independent thinker. The Instrumental Enrichment program is . . (aimed at) . . the process of learning itself. For this reason, the various components of the program have been deliberately called "instruments" and the entire program "Instrumental Enrichment." The contents around which each instrument is built serve only as a vehicle for the development, refinement, and crystallization of the functional prerequisites of thinking. Implicit in the conception of Instrumental Enrichment*
>
> (continued on next page)

is the conviction that manifest low cognitive performance need not be regarded as a stable characteristic of an individual and that systematic intervention, directed at the correction of deficient functions, will render the condition reversible by producing a change in the cognitive structure of the individual."

Source: Feuerstein, R. & Jensen M. 1980. Instrumental Enrichment: Theoretical basis, goals and instruments, *Educational Forum*, 44, no. 4:401-23.

"The overall aim of the Instrumental Enrichment exercises is to turn children with a reduced ability to be modified—to learn and adapt—into much more flexible and reflective operators in the world. By changing and enriching a child's structure of thinking, Instrumental Enrichment makes him/her more receptive to stimuli and experience, and increasingly able to cope with new conditions and situations confronting him/her in life and, of course, in school."

Source: [page 96] Sharron, H. 1987. *Changing children's minds: Feuerstein's revolution in the teaching of intelligence.* London: Souvenir Press.

Children's reactions to Instrumental Enrichment:

"It's brilliant for your brains."

"It helps you not to be impulsive—before I used to rush into things."

"It helped me not to be frightened of new things."

"It helped me to think."

"It helped me do my other lessons."

Source: [page 95] Sharron, H. 1987. *Changing children's minds: Feuerstein's revolution in the teaching of intelligence.* London: Souvenir Press.

Comments from pre-service teachers about Instrumental Enrichment:

"It gives me insight into the process underlying students' thinking."

"It shows how to ask questions and accept there is more than one answer."

"More of this enrichment is needed."

"It should be introduced at High School."

"I have found different and alternative ways of looking at and doing things . . ."

"It has helped me try more approaches to problems, rather than just focusing on answers."

Source: Skuy, M., Lomofsky, L., Green, & Fridjhon, P. 1993. Effectiveness of IE for pre-service teachers in a disadvantaged South African community. *International Journal of Cognitive Education and Mediated Learning*, 1(3): 92–109.

The Aim of This Book

The aim of *Bridging Learning In and Out of the Classroom* is to further elaborate and bridge the thinking skills presented in Feuerstein's Instrumental Enrichment (IE) program.

This book provides an introduction to Feuerstein's program and an explanation of what it is, why it is important, and when and where it is used. The book then offers suggestions for bridging or transcending these thinking skills into the following areas:

- the school—where examples are given in classroom situations in terms of specific subject content, to show how classroom experiences can be used to mediate thinking skills

- the home—where everyday activities in the home can be used to teach thinking skills

- the community—where suggestions are given in community/counseling situations, to show how thinking skills can be used to promote interpersonal and affective (emotional/motivational) development, enhance creativity, and facilitate multicultural awareness

The Format of This Book

The format for all fourteen chapters within *Bridging Learning In and Out of the Classroom* is the same. Each chapter deals with one thinking skill/cognitive operation. The outline for each chapter is as follows:

- Feuerstein's heading and logo or symbol for the thinking skill or instrument (See the logos for the fourteen instruments on pages xii–xiii.)//
- An explanation of the logo
- A link to the cognitive functions
  [Note: The link is set in italics in the Strategy feature at the beginning of each chapter.]
- A description of the thinking skill, why it is important, and when and where it is used
- Bridging suggestions for the school
- Bridging suggestions for the community, including counseling, affective, creative, and multicultural dimensions
- Bridging suggestions for the home
- Work pages to develop and apply ideas suggested in the chapter

SkyLight Training and Publishing Inc.

Instrumental Enrichment (IE) Instruments

1. **Organization of Dots**

2. **Comparisons**

3. **Orientation in Space I**

4. **Analytic Perception**

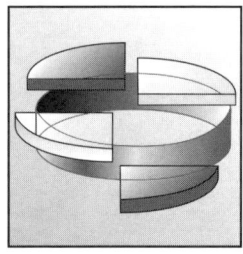

5. **Categorization**

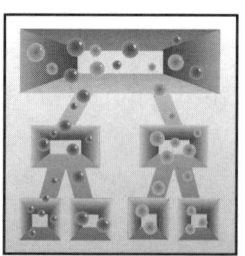

6. **Illustrations**

7. **Family Relations**

8. **Temporal Relations**

SkyLight Training and Publishing Inc.

9. **Orientation in Space II**

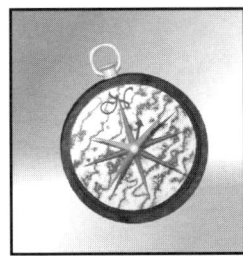

10. **Instructions**

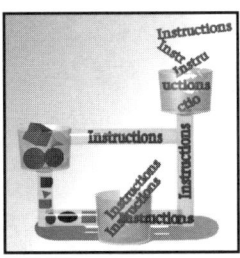

11. **Numerical Progressions**

12. **Transitive Relations**

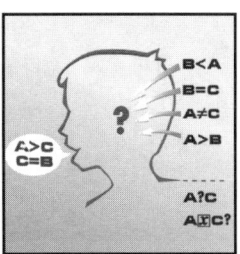

13. **Syllogisms**

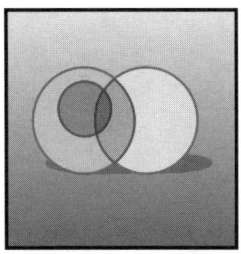

14. **Representational Stencil Design**

Note:

1. *Bridging Learning In and Out of the Classroom* is meant to be used as a companion to and not a substitute for Feuerstein's Instrumental Enrichment (IE) program.
2. Suggestions for bridging to the school, home, and community are made by way of exemplification. Other bridging examples can be found in the Instrumental Enrichment teacher guides or may be generated by the user.

CHAPTER 1

The Organization of Dots instrument focuses on the cognitive operation of organization. Feuerstein's symbol for the instrument is a group of stars in the sky which humankind has organized into recognizable and distinguishable patterns. We impose order by connecting certain stars with imaginary lines to create visual formations such as the Big Dipper (a constellation of stars found in the Northern Hemisphere).

Organization of Dots

Organization of Dots

STRATEGY

Understanding organization depends on the development and use of various cognitive functions.

For example, to organize a lesson we need to ensure that we have all the relevant information (clear and systematic data-gathering), *which is prepared in a structured and meaningful way* (appropriate planning, behavior, adequate elaboration of concepts, summative behavior) *and mediated in an interesting and appropriate manner* (appropriate expressive behavior).

Why is a telephone directly organized from A to Z? In what section of the supermarket would you look for the soap? How is a study timetable planned? Being able to answer these kinds of questions depends on the ability to *organize*.

Imagine a child born into this world of stimuli without the relationship between them being explored and explained. The world would appear a very confusing, chaotic, and frightening place for the child who would then experience what Feuerstein calls an "episodic grasp of reality" (the perception of reality as consisting of separate, isolated, and unrelated episodes). In order to overcome this chaos or episodic reality, we impose an order on the universe by organizing objects and events according to relationships and rules.

This kind of organization varies depending on such factors as culture. For example, writing is organized in some cultures from right to left, and in other cultures from left to right. As organization is mediated to the child, culture is transmitted. Thus, the child is able to see relationships among things and make order out of apparent chaos.

What Is Organization?

Organization involves forming relationships among objects, events, or ideas according to rules, systems, principles, or criteria. For example, words in a dictionary are organized in alphabetical order.

Why Is Organization Important?

- to aid understanding (e.g., an essay having greater clarity when it is organized into an introduction, body, and conclusion)
- to create order and meaning (e.g., laws of the land being organized into a legal system so that people understand their rights)
- for efficiency (e.g., diaries or daily logs, which enable us to manage time more productively)
- for convenience (e.g., products in a discount or superstore being organized into departments, such as groceries, kitchenware, gardening tools, and clothing to make shopping easier

When and Where Do We Organize?

- Time can be organized into seconds, minutes, hours, days, weeks, seasons, years, centuries, etc.
- Objects are arranged according to criteria (e.g., food in a shop, books in a library, clothes in a closet).
- Activities are planned and arranged (e.g., outings, parties, tournaments, games).
- Ideas and thoughts need formulating and structuring (e.g., poems, mind maps or overviews, arguments).
- Knowledge can be categorized (e.g., science, fine arts, humanities).

BRIDGING

In the School

NUMEROUS CLASSROOM EXPERIENCES CAN BE USED TO MEDIATE **ORGANIZATION**. FOLLOWING ARE SOME EXAMPLES:

GENERAL
- ☐ Improve study skills. For example, apply organizational principles to organize a study timetable, a workplace, and the particular subject content.
- ☐ Develop a plan that can always be used to check or proofread written work.
- ☐ Summarize course work in a mind map or overview.

LANGUAGE ARTS
- ☐ Become familiar with the way a dictionary is organized in order to use it more effectively.
- ☐ Organize an essay into introduction, body, and conclusion.
- ☐ Mediate how spelling is organized in terms of word families, prefixes and suffixes, etc.

HISTORY
- ☐ Create time lines to illustrate the order of historical events.
- ☐ Make a history presentation more creative by planning how you could use models, charts, maps, illustrations, etc.
- ☐ Examine the sequence of historical events based on cause and effect.

GEOGRAPHY
- ☐ Use maps (such as political, physical, topical or contour maps) to illustrate how land, people, and resources can be organized.
- ☐ Show how imaginary lines represent the organization of land (equator, tropics), time zones, ocean currents, wind, weather fronts, and stars (constellations).

GENERAL SCIENCE
- ☐ Organize an experiment (e.g., aim, apparatus, hypothesis, method, result, conclusion).
- ☐ Examine how ecosystems are organized into food chains, life cycles, etc.
- ☐ Discuss the organization of body systems (e.g., the human respiratory system, digestive system, etc.).

MATH
- ☐ Graph statistical data into pie graphs, line graphs, or bar graphs.
- ☐ Show how numerical values can be placed into columns (e.g., 10s, 100s, other units of measurement, etc.).
- ☐ Show how positive and negative numbers can be organized on a number line.

FINE ARTS
- ☐ Follow a plan in order to complete some art processes effectively (e.g., scupturing, photographing, painting, silkscreening, etc.).
- ☐ Look at how a painting is organized in order to aid art appreciation.
- ☐ Compare how space is organized differently in various architectural periods.

Organization of Dots

BRIDGING

In the Home

EVERYDAY ACTIVITIES CAN BE USED TO TEACH THE SKILL OF **ORGANIZATION**.

Everyday activities in the home can be used to teach the skill of organization. Make a mundane shopping trip more meaningful by mediating to children how and why the products in a supermarket have been organized. For example, show how perishables are stored in refrigerated sections of the store and cleaning products are separated from food. Encourage children to use these principles of organization when unpacking the purchases back home.

Encourage family involvement in the organization of a hiking trip. This involves several levels of planning and organization. For example, a day-by-day itinerary needs to be formulated and coordinated with a menu plan. A checklist of food and equipment should be devised and the purchasing of these items organized. Other factors to consider would be roles and responsibilities among participants, transportation arrangements, packing procedures, fitness training, provisions for first aid, etc.

Other occasions when organization can be mediated include
- ☐ setting the table
- ☐ following a recipe
- ☐ organizing furniture in a room or in a doll house
- ☐ following rules of a game (e.g., Scrabble)
- ☐ arranging a party
- ☐ managing money
- ☐ organizing photos from a holiday or vacation in a photo album
- ☐ explaining sections of the newspaper
- ☐ finding books in a library

In the Community

BRIDGING

ORGANIZATION IS A SKILL THAT CAN BE USED TO PROMOTE INTERPERSONAL AND AFFECTIVE (EMOTIONAL) DEVELOPMENT, ENHANCE CREATIVITY, AND FACILITATE MULTICULTURAL AWARENESS.

COUNSELING

Organize your thoughts in decision making.
- For example, examine the pros and cons of all the alternatives before making a final choice.

Develop an understanding as to how institutions and bureaucracies are organized.
- For example, explore organizations in terms of hierarchies, power structures, or rules and regulations.

AFFECTIVE

Disorganization can lead to negative emotions such as anger, frustration, and low self-esteem; and feeling "swamped," "bogged-down," and generally unable to cope. Consider organization as a remedy for disorganization.

Organization of Dots

In the Community

BRIDGING

ORGANIZATION IS A SKILL THAT CAN BE USED TO PROMOTE INTERPERSONAL AND AFFECTIVE DEVELOPMENT, ENHANCE CREATIVITY, AND FACILITATE MULTICULTURAL AWARENESS.

CREATIVE

There are many creative activities that can develop organizational skills.

"There was an old woman who lived in a shoe. She had so many children, she didn't know what to do. . . ."

Design and organize a "shoe-house" for the old woman in the familiar nursery rhyme, a place that will accommodate the needs of all the children.

MULTICULTURAL

ORGANIZATION can be used to promote empathy and appreciation of different cultures.

A day in the life of . . .

Experience a day with a colleague or friend from a different country or culture. Observe how that individual's day is organized. For example, experience or observe

- events of the day
- structure of religious or social rituals
- preparation of meals
- family hierarchy or home situations

Record your observations and feelings and apply your organizational skills to put together a presentation of your experience.

SkyLight Training and Publishing Inc.

WORK PAGE

TRUE OR FALSE?

Give reasons for your answer.

1. Organized material is better remembered than bits and pieces of unrelated information.

2. The skill of organization can assist in overcoming an episodic grasp of reality.

BRIDGING

Design a strategy or plan that will help you become more organized in your field of study.

Organization of Dots

WORK PAGE

APPLICATION

Use this page to develop the ideas suggested in chapter 1.

CHAPTER 2

The Comparisons instrument focuses on the cognitive operation of comparison, such as looking for similarities and differences between items according to relevant and appropriate criteria. Feuerstein's symbol for the instrument is two circular figures that have both similar and different attributes. By mentally superimposing one figure over the other, we are able to identify which attributes are similar and which are different.

For example, both figures are circles and therefore are similar in shape, but they have their colors located in different positions—the one on the left is white on black and the one on the right is black on white.

Comparisons

Comparisons

STRATEGY

Understanding Comparisons depends on the development and use of various cognitive functions.

For example, when making a comparison of different careers, we need to take into account various factors (considering more than one source of information) *in order to make sound judgments* (addressing the need for logical evidence) *and systematically test job opportunities* (working through output responses).

How is option a related to option b? Which is the better? Which should I choose? What decision should I make?

The ability to answer these kinds of questions depends on the ability to compare. Comparison forms the basis of relational thinking—determining how objects, events, and stimuli are similar and/or different.

An effective comparison depends on the relevance of the criteria chosen. For example, if you want to compare cars in order to decide on which one to buy, the criterion of color might not be as relevant as the criterion of cost.

What Are Comparisons?

Comparison is identifying and describing the similarities and differences between objects, events, or ideas according to critical or relevant criteria. For example, if in putting together pieces of a puzzle, a black square and a black triangle are compared, the critical criterion for describing difference is shape, whereas the critical criterion for describing similarity is color.

Why Are Comparisons Important?

- to move beyond merely describing events, objects, or feelings in life and by making links and meaningful connections (e.g., happy, elated, and ecstatic denoting *different* intensities on the *same* continuum of happiness)
- to facilitate decision making by weighing the pros and cons of an argument or by prioritizing criteria used when making a choice between items (e.g., when choosing whom to vote for, the candidate's opinions may be more important than his or her political party)

When and Where Do We Compare?

- in self-expression (e.g., by defining in what ways you are the same as and different from others)
- in everyday life (e.g., by examining characteristics of food and the requirements of preparation in deciding what to cook)
- in making major life decisions (e.g., choosing what career to follow, whether to get married, where to live)
- in celebrating the diversity of cultures in a society and learning to tolerate differences in social practices
- in categorizing (e.g., grouping things according to a common attribute)

BRIDGING

In the School

NUMEROUS CLASSROOM EXPERIENCES CAN BE USED TO MEDIATE **COMPARISONS**. FOLLOWING ARE SOME EXAMPLES:

GENERAL
- Compare and evaluate different teaching techniques (e.g., cooperative learning versus individual learning).
- Compare and evaluate different approaches to taking notes in class (e.g., mind mapping versus taking notes in linear style).
- Enrich vocabulary by mediating the degrees of comparison to enable precise and accurate descriptions of objects or happenings.

LANGUAGE ARTS
- Compare characters in literature according to their values, ambitions, and personalities.
- Compare poems according to themes, style, period, imagery, and so on.
- Discuss figures of speech that are based on comparison (e.g., similes, metaphors).

HISTORY
- Compare time periods in history (e.g., the Stone Age and Iron Age according to relevant criteria, such as lifestyles, work tools, etc.).
- Critically evaluate the particular bias of opposing political perspectives in history (e.g., different writers' views of an event).
- Compare the ideologies of different political leaders or historical heroes or heroines.

GEOGRAPHY
- Draw comparison charts of different geographical phenomena (e.g., weather, seasons, mountain ranges, plant life).
- Discuss the structures of different types of communities (e.g., urban and rural).
- Use graphs to compare changing weather conditions (e.g., temperature, barometric pressure, humidity).

GENERAL SCIENCE
- Compare animal groups according to relevant criteria (e.g., locomotion, reproduction).
- Evaluate experiments by comparing the conditions and results of experimental and control groups.
- Present the arguments for and against different theories of the creation and evolution of the universe.

MATH
- Use the concepts of "greater than" and "less than" to introduce comparisons in math.
- Discuss the similarities and differences between multiplication and addition or between division and subtraction.
- Compare geometrical shapes according to relevant criteria (e.g., number of sides, angles, properties).

FINE ARTS
- Encourage art appreciation by comparing techniques of different artists or of different periods of art.
- Compare the strategies of marketing communication (e.g., writing advertising copy).
- Develop an understanding of music by comparing different selections according to criteria such as pitch, pace, instrumentation, etc.

Comparisons

BRIDGING

In the Home

EVERYDAY ACTIVITIES IN THE HOME CAN BE USED TO TEACH THE SKILL OF **COMPARISONS**.

Enrich outdoor activities by extending an understanding of nature through comparing. For example, compare the needs of different plants—whether they need plenty of sun or water—so that you know where best to plant them to determine which plant varieties attract more insects and birds. You can build up a scrapbook with pictures from magazines and newspapers to illustrate a table of the differences and similarities between all the plants in your garden.

Allow mishaps or problems to become an opportunity for creative decision making. For example, if you're preparing to fry eggs sunnyside up for breakfast and you accidently break the yolks, generate as many solutions to the problem as possible (e.g., make scrambled eggs or an omelet instead). Consider and compare the pros and cons of various alternatives in order to make the most appropriate decision.

Other occasions when Comparisons can be mediated include
- card games such as Concentration and Old Maid
- stacking pots from biggest to smallest
- comparing products in terms of value for money
- odd-one-out games such as spotting the weed among the flowers
- practice in recognizing opposites such as night/day, cold/hot, sweet/sour, hard/soft, clean/dirty, angry/happy

In the Community

BRIDGING

COMPARISON IS A SKILL THAT CAN BE USED TO PROMOTE INTERPERSONAL AND AFFECTIVE DEVELOPMENT, ENHANCE CREATIVITY, AND FACILITATE MULTICULTURAL AWARENESS.

COUNSELING

Decision Making
- For example, comparing different aspects of careers allows one to make an informed decision.

Problem Solving
- For example, comparison of positive and negative factors, using various criteria, facilitates thinking through community problems, such as whether a new park or supermarket should be built in the neighborhood; thus, in proposing a park, a criterion such as space may be listed, and the pros and cons of using available space may be discussed.

AFFECTIVE

Design an activity that will allow the individual to express differences in his or her emotional make-up (e.g., a feeling collage or a "feelie wheel").

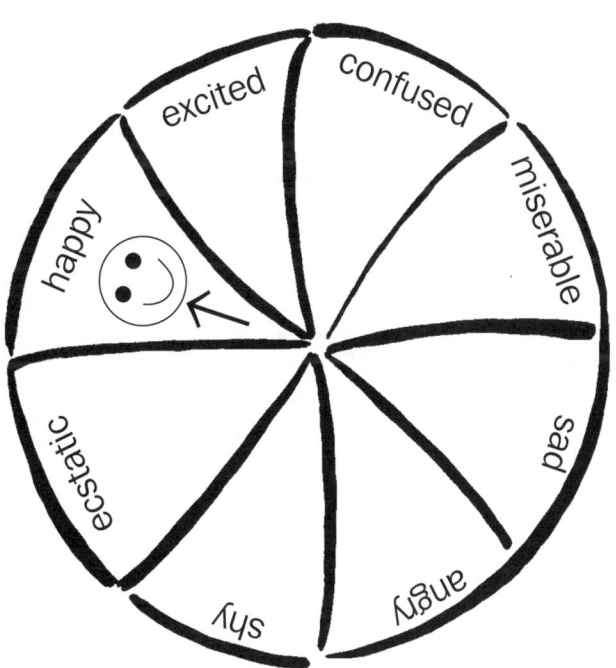

Comparisons enable individuals to identify and express the diversity of their personal feelings and help them accept differences in their emotional responses.

Comparisons

BRIDGING

In the Community

CREATIVE

There are many forms of Comparisons that can enrich creative thinking. The act of comparing can aid imagination.

Super Statues

Imagine you are a dying tree. Describe your experience.

MULTICULTURAL

A cultural treasure chest

Explore the diversity and richness of the different cultures in your community and compare them according to set criteria using a comparison table such as the one that follows. Complete the last column with another culture.

CRITERIA	AFRIKAANS	ZULU	GREEK	
FOOD	Koek-sister (braids of fried dough)	Magwinya (dough fried in fish oil)	Baklava (honey-and-nut pastry)	
GAMES	Bok-Bok (leap-frog)	Ingedo (jacks played with stones)	Piato pefao (Plate throwing)	
DRESS	Veld skoen (hiking boot)	Beshu (a decorative sash)	Forstella (a long skirt)	

WORK PAGE

TRUE OR FALSE?

Give reasons for your answer.

1. Comparison involves finding similarities and differences according to relevant and appropriate criteria.

   _____
   _____
   _____
   _____

2. Comparison specifically involves establishing the similarities between objects, events, and ideas.

   _____
   _____
   _____
   _____

BRIDGING

List the differences and similarities of attributes and skills required in various careers.

_____
_____
_____
_____
_____
_____
_____
_____

Comparisons

WORK PAGE

APPLICATION

Use this page to develop the ideas suggested in chapter 2.

CHAPTER 3

The Orientation in Space I instrument deals with the cognitive operation of understanding how objects relate to one another in space. Feuerstein's symbol for this instrument is a crossroad from which four arrows point in four different directions. It introduces the terms left, right, back, and front. The tasks show how direction, orientation, and relationships in space are relative to individual positions.

Orientation in Space I

Orientation in Space I

STRATEGY

Orientation in Space I depends on the development and use of various cognitive functions.

For example, to orientate ourselves in reading a map, we would need to understand the relative concepts of left and right (understanding spatial concepts) *and mentally transfer directions* (projecting virtual relations) *so we can follow the directions precisely* (accurate data output).

Which is the quickest route to town? Where is the fiction section of the library? If I turned 45 degrees to the right, what would be in front of me and behind me? Being able to answer these kinds of questions depends on having a good Orientation in Space I. This means that you have an internalized system of reference for describing objects and events in space.

"Oriented" can be described as having an understanding of one's relative position or being familiar with one's surroundings (the opposite of being disoriented).

"Space" can be described as an expanse or area in which objects exist or move. It includes the individual's immediate surroundings, the classroom, school, town, world, universe . . ., extending ever outwards in three dimensions.

Orientation in Space I at this "outer" or "physical" level can be bridged to an "inner" or "psychological" level. At this level, questions can be asked, such as What is your perspective on this issue? What is your point of view? How would I see things if I put myself in your shoes? Being able to answer these questions depends on one's empathy—the ability to move beyond one's personal perspective and understand things from another's point of view.

What Is Orientation in Space I?

Orientation in Space I enables us to describe relationships among objects and among events in space. It involves developing an internalized reference system (such as one's own left, right, back, and front) in order to locate oneself in space. Orientation is

- being able to organize your physical environment
- being aware of and flexible in your psychological orientation—understanding your own perspective *and* seeing things from a different perspective

Why Is Orientation in Space I Important?

- to develop relational thinking—to understand that relationships between things are relative (e.g., if I turn 90 degrees left, then what was on my *left* is now on my *right*)
- to develop metacognition or awareness of one's own and other's perspective, thinking, or feeling about something
- to develop empathic thinking or empathy, which involves seeing things from another's point of view—or putting yourself in someone else's shoes

When and Where Do We Use Orientation in Space I?

- physical orientation (e.g., reading maps or moving about in an area without causing accidents)
- psychological orientation (e.g., listening to someone else's point of view, or appreciating how historical facts can be reported from opposing viewpoints

BRIDGING

In the School

NUMEROUS CLASSROOM EXPERIENCES CAN BE USED TO MEDIATE **ORIENTATION IN SPACE I**. FOLLOWING ARE SOME EXAMPLES:

GENERAL
- Discuss the feeling of *disorientation* when in unfamiliar surroundings.
- Use games to find directions from different starting points.
- Practice changing one's orientation by describing different points of view.

LANGUAGE ARTS
- Identify prepositions that indicate a specific orientation (e.g., in, on, over, under).
- Appreciate literature through exploring the different characters' perspectives.
- Encourage the use of precise vocabulary when giving directions or explaining one's point of view.

HISTORY
- Describe and discuss political terms (e.g., left wing and right wing, liberal and conservative).
- Discuss different experiences of a historical event.
- Highlight the biases of different historians, writers, or journalists in describing events.

GEOGRAPHY
- Explain the route traveled to and from school everyday.
- Draw maps from different orientations in space (e.g., aerial views).
- Explore the changing position of the planets relative to the sun, Earth, etc.

GENERAL SCIENCE
- Draw diagrams of animals and plants from different orientations (e.g., a cross-section; transverse section, etc.).
- Discuss the theory of relativity.
- Use vectors to show magnitude and direction of motion.

MATH
- Discuss how you can use angles (e.g., 90 degrees, 180 degrees) to explain a position in space.
- Illustrate directionality using a number line (e.g., positive and negative numbers).
- Explain how the position of numbers gives them their value (e.g., hundreds, tens and other units; .01 as opposed to .1).

FINE ARTS
- Draw the same object from four different perspectives.
- Develop an understanding of the concept of symmetry.
- Encourage independent interpretations of works of art.

SkyLight Training and Publishing Inc.

Orientation in Space I

BRIDGING

In the Home

EVERYDAY ACTIVITIES CAN BE USED TO TEACH THE SKILL OF **ORIENTATION IN SPACE I**.

Create a game that involves remembering the route between your home and various other locations you often visit, such as your school, local shops, the homes of your grandparents, or the homes of friends.

In one game you can play at home, everyone can shut his or her eyes and try to imagine a particular route—who can recall the most landmarks along the way?

Another game can be played on a large sheet of paper on the floor. Draw different routes in different colors and devise symbols for the various landmarks along the way.

Other occasions when Orientation in Space I can be mediated include
- ☐ putting on the left and right shoes correctly (physical orientation)
- ☐ arranging place settings at the dining-room or kitchen table
- ☐ following sequences in dancing, karate, soccer, etc.
- ☐ creating an understanding environment with other people in the household (psychological orientation)
- ☐ creating an awareness of and caring for the needs of any pets in the household

BRIDGING

In the Community

SKILLS DEVELOPED IN THE **ORIENTATION IN SPACE I** INSTRUMENT CAN BE APPLIED TO THE RELATIONAL, HYPOTHETICAL, AND EMPATHIC THINKING NEEDED IN COUNSELING AND MULTICULTURAL INTERACTION, AS WELL AS IN AFFECTIVE AND CREATIVE THOUGHT.

COUNSELING

☐ family therapy and conflict resolution (For instance, each individual assumes a role and discusses his or her role and perceptions of others in the family setting. Individuals can explore how realistic and fair their expectations are of each other. An individual can assume the role usually taken by another family member in order to appreciate the perspective both of that family member and himself/herself.)

AFFECTIVE

Students who have strong relationships form pairs. Each member of the pair discusses how he or she views the other. Partners then compare their views. Have they been fair to each other?

Orientation in Space I

BRIDGING

In the Community

CREATIVE

There are many creative activities (physical as well as mental) that can develop a sense of Orientation in Space I.

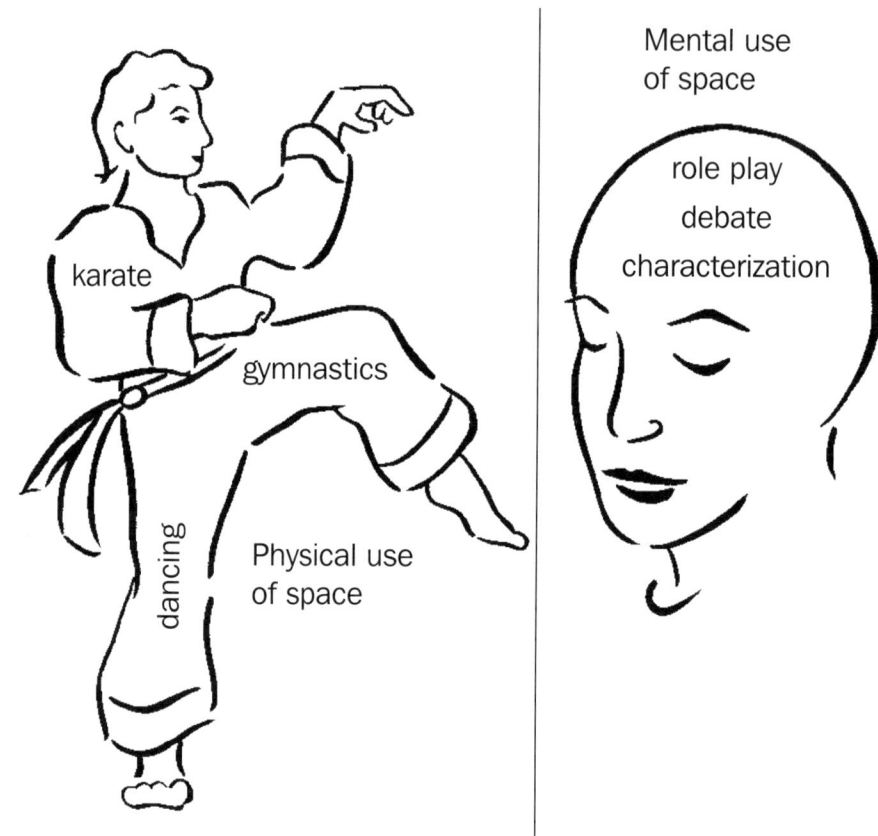

MULTICULTURAL

About my culture . . .

Select three individuals to represent three different cultures in North America today. Ask them to identify with that culture and describe issues such as the following:

- ☐ family structures (single-parent households, "traditional" families, etc.)
- ☐ women's roles
- ☐ place of and attitude toward the elderly in society
- ☐ political or socioeconomic status of the group within society

WORK PAGE

TRUE OR FALSE?

Give reasons for your answer.

1. The act of hypothesizing and predicting possible outcomes begins when the individual is able to detach himself or herself from a concrete representation of space.

   _____
   _____
   _____
   _____

2. Sympathetic understanding or insight is based on the individual's ability to transcend his or her personal space and to act on the world in an internalized, representational way.

   _____
   _____
   _____
   _____

BRIDGING

How would you use the concepts underlying Orientation in Space to illustrate to young children the importance of shifting perspectives?

_____
_____
_____
_____
_____
_____

SkyLight Training and Publishing Inc.

Orientation in Space I

BRIDGING

APPLICATION

Use this page to develop the ideas suggested in chapter 3.

CHAPTER 4

The Analytic Perception instrument focuses on the skill of breaking the whole into its parts (analysis) and putting the parts together to make a whole (synthesis). Feuerstein's symbol for this instrument is an ellipse that has been divided into four equal quarters. It introduces the skill of dividing wholes into parts according to relevant criteria.

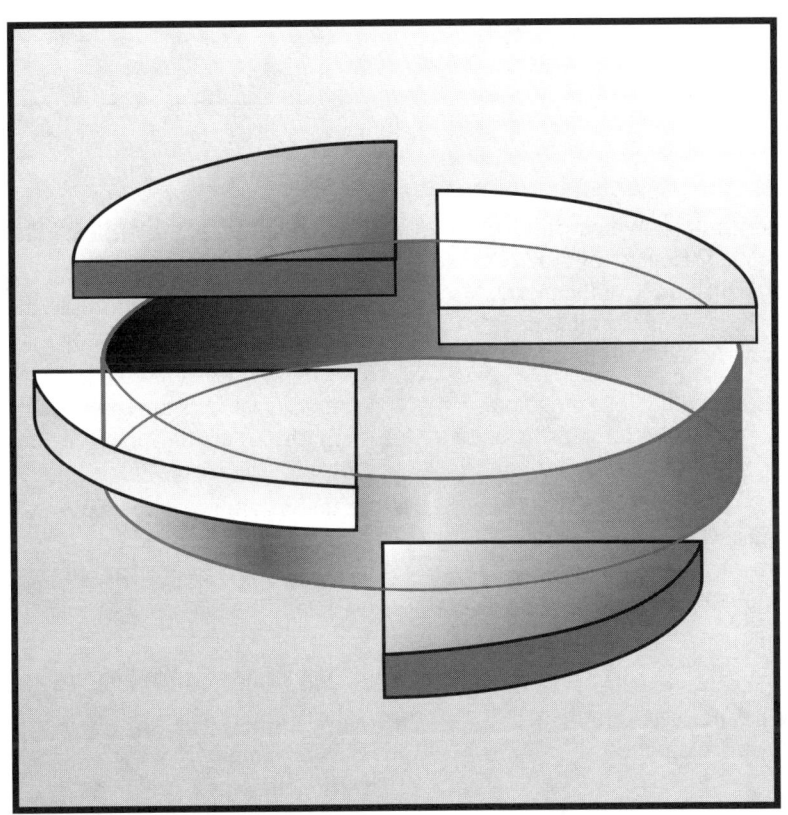

Analytic Perception

Analytic Perception

STRATEGY

Analytic Perception depends on the development and use of various cognitive functions.

For example, to write a good essay we need to break the topic into its components parts, which may involve being able to follow a sequence of events (understanding of temporal concepts), *linking cause and effect* (meaningful grasp of reality), *and using appropriate and descriptive language* (adequate expressive verbal tools).

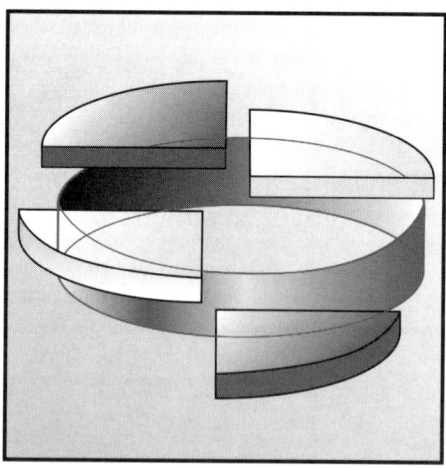

How can I fix this broken tool? Which paint colors must I mix to get green? How many study hours are there in a day? Which piece of the puzzle fits where? The ability to solve these kinds of problems depends on the ability to analyze and synthesize.

Analytic Perception involves asking the following questions: "What are the parts?" "What are the steps involved in the process?" and "How are the parts related to each other and to the whole?"

- Analysis involves dividing a whole into its parts according to relevant criteria (differentiation).
- Synthesis involves joining the parts together to make a meaningful whole (integration).

In order to adapt and function successfully in the world, we need to develop a good balance between the two processes of differentiation and integration.

What Are Analysis and Synthesis?

Analysis involves breaking up an organized whole so that the parts stand out and are separate from each other (e.g., identifying the nouns and verbs in a sentence).

Synthesis involves organizing the parts into a meaningful whole or restructuring the parts into a new and original whole (e.g., in dressmaking or assembling a model airplane).

Why Are Analysis and Synthesis Important?

- Overgeneralized perception (an ability to see the parts in the whole) leads to confused thinking (e.g., confusing *their* and *there*; confusing individual behavior with cultural characteristics).
- Complex problems are more easily solved by breaking them up and taking "one step at a time" (e.g., a story problem).
- An understanding of the parts and how they relate gives us an understanding of the whole (e.g., a mechanic can repair a car only by understanding how each part functions and how the parts fit together).

When and Where Do We Analyze and Synthesize?

- to find a single part in a whole (e.g., finding the relevant paragraph in a story, a telephone number in the directory, or a street on a map)
- to add all the parts to make a whole (e.g., following a cookie recipe, knitting squares to make a patchwork quilt, or assembling a puzzle)
- to understand the relationship between the parts and the whole (e.g., identifying the sound made by each instrument in an orchestra and seeing how the instruments combine to create a symphony; understanding how each piece of litter contributes to environmental pollution; realizing how each individual vote adds up to majority rule in a government body)

BRIDGING

In the School

NUMEROUS CLASSROOM EXPERIENCES CAN BE USED TO MEDIATE **ANALYTIC PERCEPTION**. FOLLOWING ARE SOME EXAMPLES:

GENERAL
- Assist students in reading difficult words by breaking them down into syllables or phonic sounds.
- Analyze essay or test questions carefully to ensure clear understanding.
- Color-code consonant blends or vowel digraphs to illustrate where and how they appear in a given text.

LANGUAGE ARTS
- Select and sequence individual scenes or events to construct a whole story.
- Analyze prose according to figures of speech (e.g., onomatopoeia, alliteration).
- Appreciate poetry through analyzing (e.g., rhythm, theme, mood, tone).

HISTORY
- Research historical events in terms of causes and results.
- Critically evaluate history texts or primary sources in order to highlight diffrent opinions resulting in a complete report.
- Show how historic events can be described in terms of a composite of different dimensions (e.g., economic, political, social, etc.).

GEOGRAPHY
- Illustrate how the world is divided (e.g., hemisphere, lines of latitude and longitude).
- Create puzzles from maps to show how continents are divided into countries.
- Analyze soil composition to identify the variety of minerals that make up a sample.

GENERAL SCIENCE
- Identify substances by labeling the various components (e.g., H_2O = two parts hydrogen and one part oxygen).
- Analyze the human body in terms of systems (e.g, skeletal system, respiratory system).

MATH
- Analyze how currency of the same value can be represented in numerous ways (e.g., $1.00 = 100 cents, a quarter = twenty-five cents).
- Identify missing information from mathematical problems.
- Divide geometric shapes into parts and record the degrees of different angles.

FINE ARTS
- See how the color wheel is built up with various color combinations (e.g., primary colors create complementary colors).
- Analyze works of art according to stylistic criteria such as form, color, line, tone, etc.
- Create a "found-art" sculpture by using litter or "trash" as the parts of the sculpture.

SkyLight Training and Publishing Inc.

Analytic Perception

BRIDGING

In the Home

EVERYDAY ACTIVITIES IN THE HOME CAN BE USED TO TEACH THE SKILL OF **ANALYTIC PERCEPTION**. FOLLOWING IS AN EXAMPLE:

Use a baking session as an exercise in analytic perception! Explain how chocolate chip cookies are made up of a combination of different ingredients (parts) mixed together in a specific sequence to make a batch of cookies (a whole). Have children go through the steps of the recipe with you—adding ingredients, stirring, and so on. Of course, don't forget about the best part—tasting the cookies after they're baked!

Provide opportunites for children to create a whole from its parts by assembling building blocks, Legos, Brio Mec toys, or puzzles. Invite children to take apart, analyze, and reassemble toys and models to form complete wholes.

Other occasions when analysis and synthesis can be mediated include
- getting dressed (e.g., selecting items of clothing to make up different outfits)
- making clothes (e.g., tailoring, assembling pattern pieces)
- designing patchwork quilts or jackets
- planning a balanced meal in terms of nutritional value
- assembling the parts of a tool or household appliance
- playing games that involve combining parts to make wholes (e.g., Scrabble, puzzles).
- mixing paints to make new colors
- explaining stages in building a house
- inviting children to observe the different roles that are played in a team game

BRIDGING

In the Community

ANALYTIC PERCEPTION SKILLS ARE NEEDED TO DIFFERENTIATE THE PARTS THAT MAKE UP SOCIAL SYSTEMS, CULTURES, AND THE SELF, SO THAT WE CAN REINTEGRATE PARTS INTO MORE MEANINGFUL, CREATIVE, AND EFFICIENT WHOLES.

COUNSELING

Explore all the factors associated with an established system.
- For example, when integrating new members into an established team, how will the new "parts" affect the existing whole?

Use analysis and synthesis in problem solving and decision making.
- For example, the strategy "thinking globally, acting locally" implies seeing a problem in its macro sense (synthesis), but dealing with the component parts in a structured micro sense (analysis).

AFFECTIVE

Children can build a collage of feelings in the form of a blanket of fabric or paper that can be hung up on the wall and shared with others.

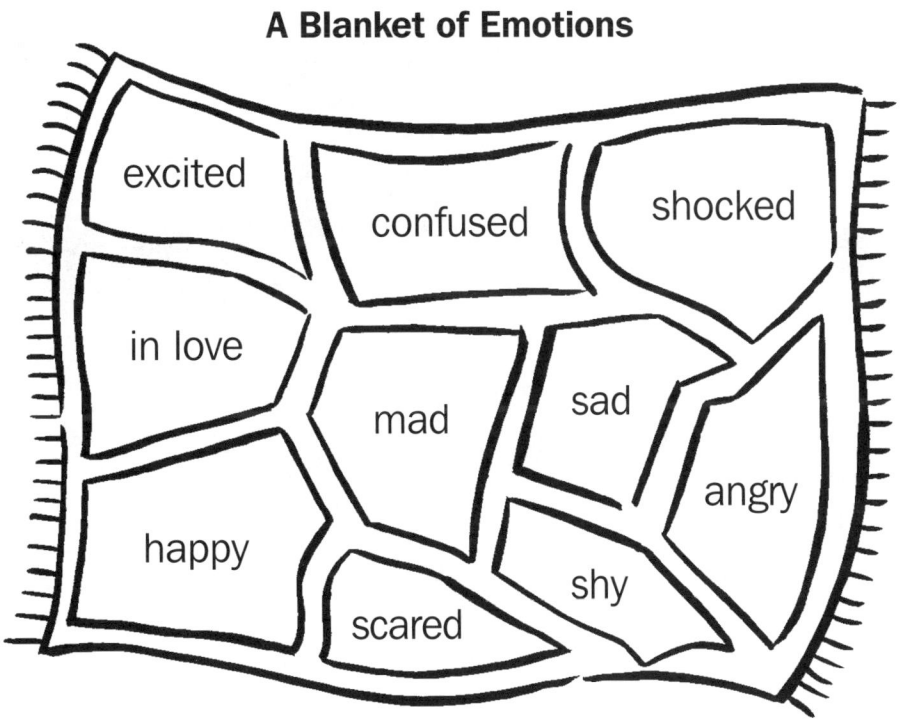

A Blanket of Emotions

Analysis of parts of the self, and synthesis of these parts into the whole unique being, can be done through various affective activities (e.g., assembling a collage reflecting personal characteristics). Such an activity will enable children to explore the multicultural aspects of their individual natures and accept them as integral parts of their personalities.

Analtyic Perception

BRIDGING

In the Community

CREATIVE

Analytical thinking can be used for the creative presentation of concrete and abstract ideas. For instance, an individual can play with a tangram (a Chinese puzzle consisting of five triangles, a square, and a rhomboid) and come up with different results.

Tangram

Make different figures from the same pieces.

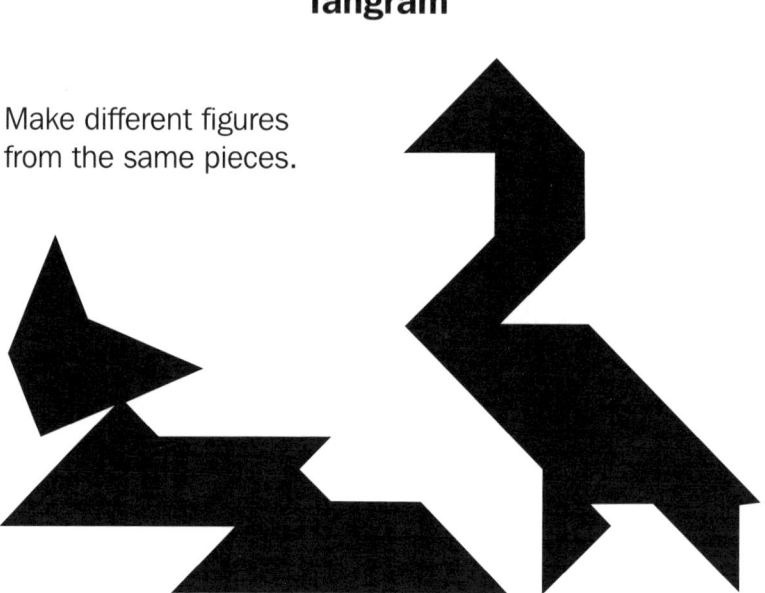

MULTICULTURAL

Analytic Perception can be used to promote empathy and appreciation of different cultures.

a cultural melting pot . . .

Imagine a pot of different cultures melting together. Analyze the customs and values of various cultures within that pot. Select those you value most in order to create a new integrated society.

Begin by discussing the following traditional customs. Would you include them in your new society?

- ☐ eating certain foods with one's hands instead of with eating utensils
- ☐ having elderly family members live with their children's families
- ☐ giving more respect and placing more importance on female members of the society or family unit
- ☐ marrying someone selected by the family

WORK PAGE

TRUE OR FALSE?

Give reasons for your answer.

1. Analytic Perception is the separation of the whole into its component parts.

   _____
   _____
   _____
   _____

2. Analytic Perception will develop an individual's internal frame of reference so that he or she is able to structure and restructure situations on his or her own.

   _____
   _____
   _____
   _____

BRIDGING

How would you use the concept of Analytic Perception to show how "the whole is more than the sum of the parts" (e.g., a person is more than a simple sum of his or her body parts)?

_____
_____
_____
_____
_____
_____
_____

Analytic Perception

WORK PAGE

APPLICATION

Use this page to develop the ideas suggested in the chapter 4.

CHAPTER 5

This instrument focuses on the cognitive operation of Categorization—grouping according to appropriate principles. Feuerstein's symbol for this instrument shows how a mixed group of circles can be divided into subgroups according to the principles of color and size. Four categories can then be created from the large, unsorted group. These subgroups of circles are small/black, large/black, large/white, and small/white. The arrows created by space at the bottom point upward and indicate that the process can be reversed to reconstruct the original group (as compared with Analytic Perception).

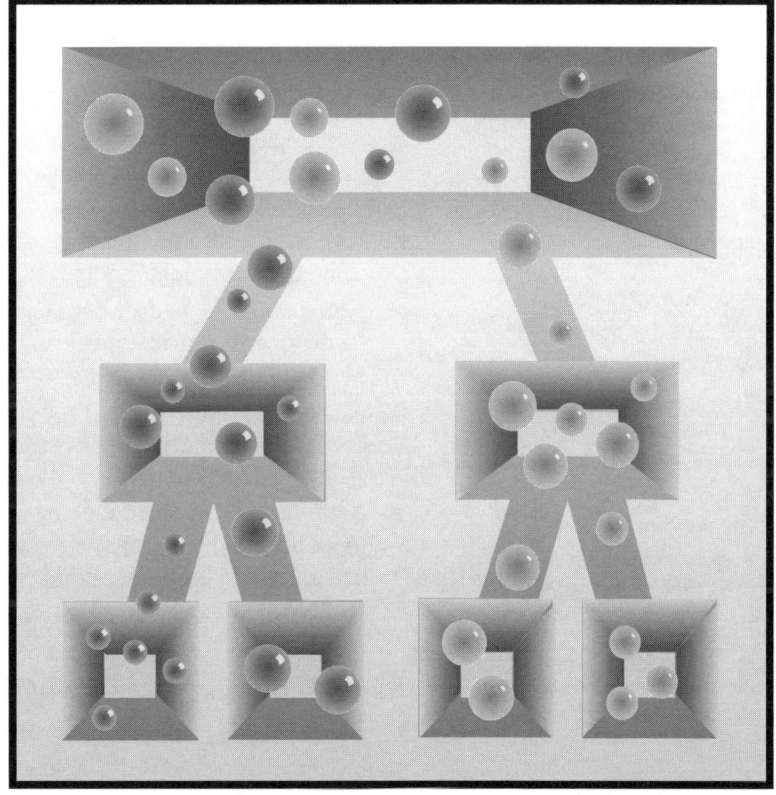

Categorization

Categorization

STRATEGY

Categorization depends on the development and use of various cognitive functions.

For example, when categorizing children into school classes we need to recognize the different characteristics of both child and teacher (consider more than one source of information) *and evaluate the circumstances under which the child will do best* (engage in spontaneous comparative behavior) *so as to minimize the chances of an incorrect placement* (trial-and-error response).

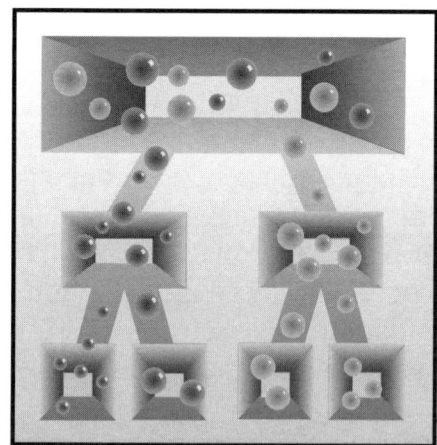

How could a student organize a mass of study notes for final exams? How does a shopper know where to find boys' clothing in a department store? According to what principles are players selected to form a soccer team? The ability to answer these kinds of questions depends on the ability to categorize.

Categorization means grouping elements according to relevant principles (e.g., sorting laundry into piles of whites, colored items, and handwashables). Such ordering makes our lives more efficient and ordered.

What Is Categorization?

Categorization builds on all the previous cognitive operations presented. It involves establishing sets based on the commonalities among elements and subsets based on the differences between members. For example, students might be grouped into a set based on the commonality of their ages, and into subsets based on their different reading abilities.

Categories are not fixed and can change depending on criteria. Categories often are not the only or even the most useful way of organizing information—in some instances, a continuum may be more relevant.

Why Is Categorization Important?

- to organize information (e.g., books in a library are organized into categories such as fiction and nonfiction)
- to remember information (e.g., constructing categorization tables of course content as an aid to studying)
- to be economical and efficient (e.g., the sections of the newspaper provides quick and easy access to information)
- to gain insight into the way society functions (e.g., when race or gender is the basis of discriminating against certain groups)
- to label categories accurately, by not overincluding or underincluding (e.g., an apple is a member of the set of food and the subset of fruit, but not the subset of vegetables)

When and Where Do We Categorize?

- in the home (e.g., packing away toys)
- in school (e.g., finding synonyms that have been grouped together in a thesaurus)
- in the community (e.g., the legal system is categorized into various subsections, such as criminal, civil, juvenile law)

BRIDGING

In the School

NUMEROUS CLASSROOM EXPERIENCES CAN BE USED TO MEDIATE **CATEGORIZATION**. FOLLOWING ARE SOME EXAMPLES:

GENERAL
- ☐ Make overviews of the course work for the year in different subjects by grouping them into main sections and subsections.
- ☐ Demonstrate, as in a workshop, how different school subjects can be categorized differently by use of other criteria.

LANGUAGE ARTS
- ☐ Group spelling words that have similar phonemes together, in order to facilitate easy recall (e.g., boat, coat, float).
- ☐ Group words that have similar meanings together (synonyms).
- ☐ Group similar parts of speech from a passage of text (e.g., grouping all the nouns and verbs, and then making subgroups (e.g., common nouns and proper nouns; state-of-being and action verbs).

HISTORY
- ☐ Tabulate information by grouping into sections (e.g., World War I can be categorized according to causes, battles, famous people, etc.).
- ☐ Teach history through themes (e.g., laws, period costumes, transportation, etc.).
- ☐ Design categorization tables to show how different political orientations can be grouped (e.g., right wing and left wing, and—within each of these—progressive or conservative).

GEOGRAPHY
- ☐ Classify regions according to their climates and natural vegetation (e.g., by use of the terms subtropical, equatorial, temperate, savanna, prairie, etc.).
- ☐ Devise a categorization table showing how the world is divided politically into continents that are divided into countries, provinces or states, cities, etc. (e.g., North America—United States—Illinois—Chicago; Africa—South Africa—Gauteng—Johannesburg).

GENERAL SCIENCE
- ☐ Discuss the classification of animals (e.g., vertebrates and invertebrates and their subgroups—mammals, reptiles, birds).
- ☐ Show how the periodic table groups elements according to their chemical properties.
- ☐ Organize substances into the three phase change of matter (e.g., solids, liquids, gases).

MATH
- ☐ Use Venn diagrams to show how members are classified into sets and subsets.
- ☐ Group numbers according to common multiples to understand multiplication tables.

FINE ARTS
- ☐ Categorize all the possible avenues or mediums of an art form (e.g., graphics—etchings, lithographs; sculpture—clay, iron; painting—oil, water).
- ☐ Group musical instruments into types (e.g., percussion, string, wind).

Categorization

BRIDGING

In the Home

EVERYDAY ACTIVITIES IN THE HOME CAN BE USED TO TEACH THE COGNITIVE OPERATION OF **CATEGORIZATION**.

While they are playing with building block toys per toy stores, encourage children to assemble the various shapes according to different criteria, such as building a tower using only the rectangular blocks (criterion of shape) or only the blue blocks (criterion of color). Extend a child's concept of categorization by combining two criteria (such as asking him or her to find a blue rectangle (criteria of color and shape).

As another activity, stimulate children's awareness of plant groups in the yard or park by identifying common characteristics (e.g., referring to trees that lose their leaves in winter as *deciduous* trees).

Other occasions when Categorization can be mediated include
- playing games which require children to identify "the odd one out of a category
- playing card games that involve matching, such as Concentration
- asking children to identify the equipment needed for a particular activity (e.g., for painting you need a brush, paint, water, paper, and a painting smock)
- sorting silverware into correct trays (i.e., knives, forks, spoons)

BRIDGING

In the Community

CATEGORIZATION CAN BE USED TO CORRELATE AND SIMPLIFY DATA-GATHERING IN PROBLEM SOLVING, COUNSELING, AND MULTICULTURAL INTERACTION AS WELL AS FOR PRESENTING INFORMATION IN BOTH THE AFFECTIVE AND CREATIVE AREAS.

COUNSELING
- Narrow down and identify groups of career options (e.g., looking at groups of careers in terms of values, interests, and abilities).
- Recognize that "smaller bits are easier to handle" (e.g., enhancing study skills by dividing data into areas that make them easier to remember and recall).

AFFECTIVE
In a vocabulary-building exercise, categorize feelings according to the kinds of intensity associated with a particular feeling. For example, consider the word *happy* and categorize it according to the values or degrees of *strong, mild,* and *weak*.

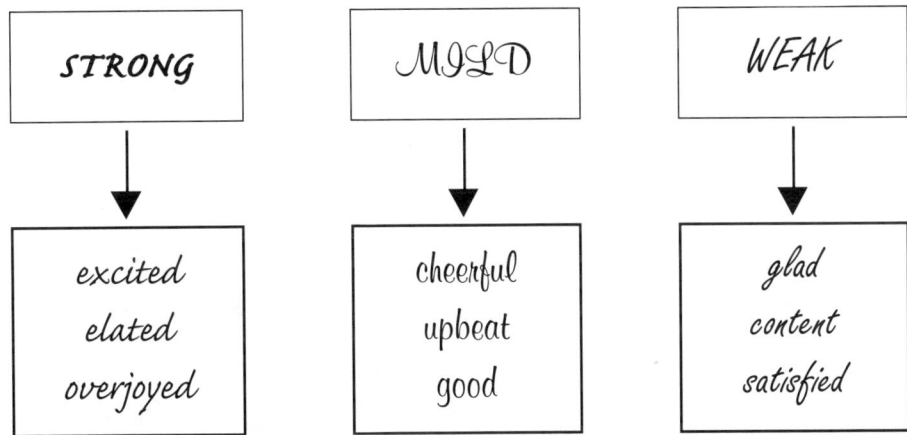

Categorizing feelings facilitates an expression of feelings by developing a "feeling" vocabulary. This aids clear communication, promotes empathy, and develops insight into the self.

CREATIVE
Categorization can be used creatively by changing the criteria for inclusion and exclusion within sets and looking for less obvious criteria. For example, consider the Twenty Questions game.

Categorization

BRIDGING

In the Community

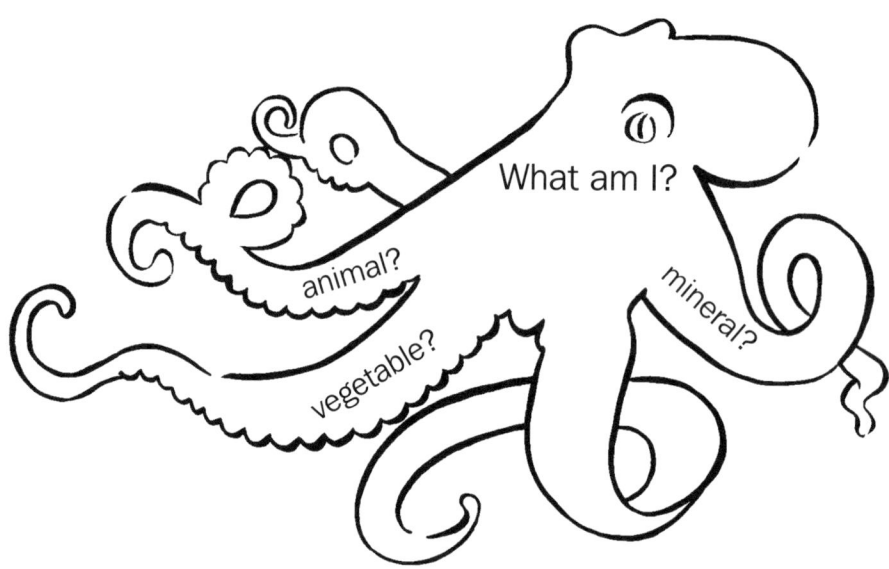

MULTICULTURAL

Categorization can be used to promote empathy for and appreciation of different cultures:

A cultural treasure hunt . . .

Set up an activity in which students research customs and values within different cultures under specific categories, such as food, music, literature, or medicine. For example, in the Orthodox Jewish religious culture, traditions are maintained through food (kosher), literature (the Torah), and music (liturgy).

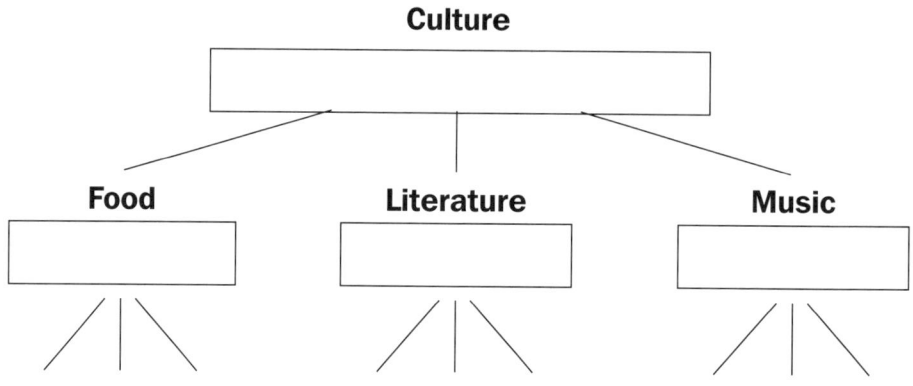

WORK PAGE

TRUE OR FALSE?

Give reasons for your answer.

1. Categorization is designed to deal with difficulties encountered by the learner in the organization of gathered data into superordinate categories.

   _____
   _____
   _____
   _____

2. In Categorization, the rule for the set is discovered through deduction and then it is applied by the process of induction.

   _____
   _____
   _____
   _____

BRIDGING

Develop a Categorization table to illustrate groupings of interests as applied to career choices.

Categorization

WORK PAGE

APPLICATION

Use this page to develop the ideas suggested in chapter 5.

CHAPTER 6

The Illustrations instrument focuses on problem solving. Reuven Feuerstein uses illustrations or cartoons to show in a humorous way why problems occur and different ways of understanding and solving them. The illustration or cartoon below shows in an absurd way the problems related to doing a job without thinking. The man mechanically painting the wall without thinking paints over another man who, also failing to think, gets painted.

Illustrations

Illustrations

STRATEGY

Problem solving depends on the development and use of various cognitive functions.

For example, to engage in effective problem solving, we need to distinguish between the essential and nonessential features of a situation (conserve constancy), *think through the nature and implications of different courses of action* (ability to internalize events), *and present the outcome in a way which makes sense to others* (mature communication skills).

Why do problems arise? Can all problems be solved directly? When does one need to use creative and ingenious solutions to problems? What can we learn from absurd or humorous situations? What values govern the solutions we choose in solving problems?

The ability to answer these kinds of questions depends first on the ability to perceive that a disequilibrium exists—to identify a problem—and second, to restore equilibrium—to provide an appropriate solution to the problem. This ability involves understanding cause-and-effect relationships (e.g., if I act impulsively, I may cause an accident to happen); being creative in solving difficult dilemmas (e.g., the problems of world pollution); examining our motives for the solutions we choose (e.g., resolving marital conflicts).

In the Illustrations instrument many humorous situations—often exaggerated and absurd—are depicted as springboards to discussing causes of problems, consequences of actions, solutions to problems, consequences of solutions, as well as moral and ethical behavior.

What Is Problem Solving?

Problem solving involves identifying cause-and-effect relationships. It begins with identifying that something is wrong and then either learning from the situation or solving it. It involves interpreting life events, making moral judgments, and acting in an innovative and ingenious way. Through problem solving we gain insight into our values and creative potential—we learn from life.

Why Is Problem Solving Important?

Problem solving can be used to teach variable educational as well as everyday life skills. In the Illustrations instrument this is done through humorous cartoons or situations. Following are examples:

- The cartoon of a man who was irritated by a hornet impulsively swatted the nest, and is now being chased by a swarm of hornets. (See page 2 of the Illustrations Student Instrument.)
- The cartoon of two yoked donkeys pulling stubbornly against each other so that neither is able to eat the corn. This illustration teaches us that the life skill of cooperation is the best way to achieve a common goal. (See page 2 of the Illustrations Student Instrument.)

When and Where Do We Use Problem Solving?

- in decision making—acting according to our value system (e.g., cheating or studying to pass a test)
- in everyday life—solving problems in a direct and straight-forward way (e.g., sorting out a confusion in communication by rephrasing a comment)
- in everyday life—solving problems indirectly and creatively (e.g., using a nylon stocking as a makeshift fan belt to get a car to the repair shop)

BRIDGING

In the School

NUMEROUS CLASSROOM EXPERIENCES CAN BE USED TO MEDIATE PROBLEM SOLVING. FOLLOWING ARE SOME EXAMPLES:

GENERAL
- ☐ Appreciate that what might be a problem to one person is not a problem to another (e.g., for some teachers a noisy classroom is a learning classroom and for others it is a disruptive home).
- ☐ Encourage independent, divergent, and autonomous solutions to problems (e.g., math problems; teacher-student conflict; writing or spelling difficulties; boredom).

LANGUAGE ARTS
- ☐ Develop debating skills (e.g., support or defend a point of view during an argument).
- ☐ Use examples in literature to evaluate problems and to problem solve (e.g., the feud in Shakespeare's *Romeo and Juliet*).

HISTORY
- ☐ Create scenarios to solve historical problems (e.g., pretending you are Albert Schweitzer solving the problems of malaria in Africa in the middle of the twentieth century).
- ☐ Use historical and contemporary newspaper cartoons to interpret political problems.

GEOGRAPHY
- ☐ Encourage students to solve environmental problems creatively (e.g., solving soil erosion, deforestation, oil spills in the ocean).
- ☐ Critically evaluate existing policies that control certain problems in terms of short-term and long-term effects (e.g., protecting endangered species, water conservation, protecting the rain forest to prevent depletion of the ozone layer in the atmosphere).

GENERAL SCIENCE
- ☐ Outline and discuss the steps involved in performing a science experiment (e.g., testing acidity—ph level—of water).
- ☐ Encourage divergent thinking in solving technological problems in supplying energy needs (e.g., wind, solar, or battery-powered engines).

MATH
- ☐ Encourage individual approaches in solving math problems (e.g., asking how many ways you can get to the sum of 45).
- ☐ Show how students can apply math concepts to problems in everyday life (e.g., problems involving mass, volume, or budgeting).

FINE ARTS
- ☐ Design user-friendly products (e.g., designing a new kind of chair in industrial arts/ vocational education class).
- ☐ Work through all the problem-solving steps in producing a play (e.g., props, costumes, music, script, lighting, staging, casting the characters, etc.).

Illustrations

BRIDGING

In the Home

EVERYDAY ACTIVITIES IN THE HOME CAN BE USED TO TEACH THE SKILL OF PROBLEM SOLVING.

Refer to page 20 in the Illustrations Student Instrument, the cartoon of two yoked donkeys pulling a cart in different directions. Showing such a cartoon can teach the concept of cooperation as a means of problem solving. This illustration can be bridged to show children the need for cooperation in order to play a team game successfully.

Through the cartoon of the Mother Dog and Her Puppies on page 5 in the Illustrations Student Instrument, demonstrate how individuality exists in a family, discussing the different ways one copes when faced with a problem.

Other occasions when problem solving can be mediated include
- seeing the funny side of situations in the home, such as in being able to laugh at oneself to release tension and to solve or prevent problems from being blown out of proportion (e.g., pancakes being flipped in a frying pan and getting stuck to the ceiling)
- making safe decisions in an emergency in the home, because impulsive solutions could exacerbate the situation (e.g., pouring water on a grease fire on the stove)

SkyLight Training and Publishing Inc.

BRIDGING

In the Community

ILLUSTRATIONS ARE A COLLECTION OF SITUATIONS IN WHICH PROBLEMS LEADING TO A DISEQUILIBRIUM ARE PERCEIVED AND RECOGNIZED. THE RESTORING OF EQUILIBRIUM CAN BE BRIDGED EFFECTIVELY TO IDENTIFY SOLUTIONS TO PROBLEMS IN COUNSELING AND MULTICULTURAL SITUATIONS. MANY OF SUCH PROBLEMS HAVE AN EMOTIVE CONTENT THAT ALLOWS EASY BRIDGING INTO THE AFFECTIVE AND CREATIVE AREAS.

COUNSELING

- ☐ Develop an awareness of cause-and-effect situations in society (e.g., the consequences of alcohol abuse or not using contraceptives).
- ☐ Illustrate the importance of being prepared and being able to improvise (having a job interview suddenly scheduled during a time when you'll be on a vacation).

AFFECTIVE

Pictures, posters, and photographs can be used as springboards for discussion of feelings, attitudes, and values.

The pictorial mode often offers a very safe environment for revealing and discussing sensitive issues (e.g., how do I feel when . . .).

Illustrations

BRIDGING

In the Community

CREATIVE

Illustrations can be used as springboards to creative activities involving lateral thinking.

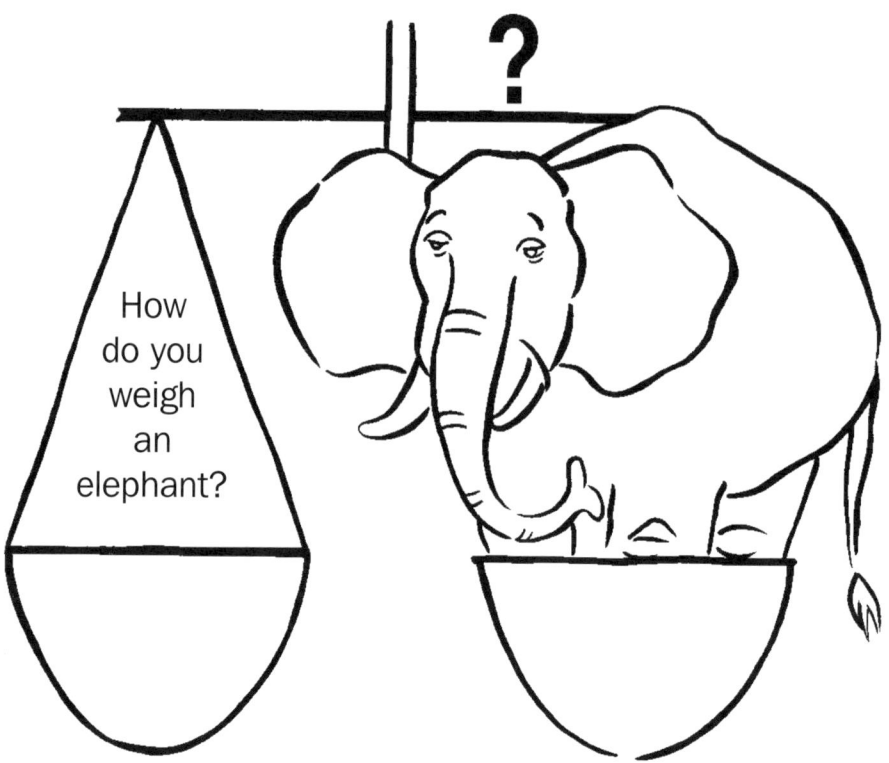

MULTICULTURAL

Cartoons can be used as a stimulus for discussion of various cultures' traditions in teams of relationships, ethics, and behavior and food.

Multicultural cuisine . . .

Create a cartoon that shows some individuals may find the traditional dishes of certain cultures, such as the following, deplorable:

☐ The Japanese eat raw fish (sushi).
☐ The Scots eat haggis, a stew cooked in the stomach of a sheep.
☐ The Malawians of Africa eat termites.
☐ The French eat snails and frog legs.

WORK PAGE

TRUE OR FALSE?

Give reasons for your answer.

1. Inferential thinking and analogical reasoning are necessary to determine the cause-and-effect situations depicted in the illustrated medium.

   _____
   _____
   _____
   _____

2. By viewing each frame of a cartoon episodically, the true relevance and meaning of the situation emerges.

   _____
   _____
   _____
   _____

BRIDGING

   Collect a group of cartoons that you could classify in terms of each of the groupings found within the instrument (Illustrations). Describe how you would bridge the illustrations to everyday situations with young children.

   _____
   _____
   _____
   _____
   _____
   _____

Illustrations

WORK PAGE

APPLICATION

Use this page to develop the ideas suggested in chapter 6.

CHAPTER 7

The Family Relations instrument focuses on inferring, understanding, and explaining relationships. Feuerstein's symbol for this instrument is a genealogical map or *genogram* that illustrates the relationships among members of a nuclear family. The squares represent males and the circles, females. This genogram describes the relationships of marriage (husband and wife) and parenthood (two sons and a daughter).

Family Relations

Family Relations

STRATEGY

Understanding Family Relations depends on the development and use of various cognitive functions.

For example, to understand the roles and relationships of people within organizations we need to understand the terminology used there (precise, accurate, and receptive verbal tools) *and the principles that govern that interaction* (inferential hypothetical thinking) *to ensure effective behavior* (participatory responses).

How is the relationship between a parent and a child different from the relationship between a husband and wife? Are all relationships permanent? Can an individual have a number of different relationships at the same time? Do relationships determine roles? The ability to answer these kinds of questions depends on the ability to understand and project relationships.

A relationship is a connection, tie, or bond between two or more objects or people. There are many different types of relationships, and an understanding of these makes us more aware of interpersonal, institutional, and societal dynamics.

What Are Family Relations?

A relationship is a certain kind of link between separate entities. The Family Relations instrument describes various kinds of links or connections (e.g., relationships by law [husband and wife], by blood [parent and child], as well as relationships that are permanent [sister] or transient [divorcees], etc.)

Why Are Family Relations Important?

- to appreciate that different kinds of relationships exist, such as direct versus indirect and horizontal versus hierarchical (e.g., a marriage is a horizontal relationship and parenthood is hierarchical)
- to understand the multiplicity of relationships an individual can have (e.g., a woman can be a mother, daughter, and wife at the same time)
- to follow the progression of relationships and realize they are not static (e.g., a mother becomes a mother-in-law)
- to serve as a symbol for other systems (e.g., school, society) and the relationships operating within them
- to provide a basis for making inferences and drawing appropriate conclusions about relationships
- to provide a basis for comparison of relationships existing within various systems

When and Where Do We Need to Describe Family Relations?

- to differentiate between various kinds of relationships (e.g., a business partnership is different from a boss-employee relationship)
- to apply the concepts involved to everyday life experiences (e.g., family of nations, systems in a business, genealogy of animals, family of nouns, etc.)

BRIDGING

In the School

NUMEROUS CLASSROOM EXPERIENCES CAN BE USED TO MEDIATE **FAMILY RELATIONS.** FOLLOWING ARE SOME EXAMPLES:

GENERAL
- ☐ Play games, such as chess, that illustrate the relationship between different players and places (e.g., in chess the Queen is more powerful than the Bishop and the pawns are equal).
- ☐ Outline a typical school hierarchy (e.g., principal—teachers—teacher aides—students) and identify relationships and roles.
- ☐ Discuss different types of relationships (e.g., friends, teacher-student).

LANGUAGE ARTS
- ☐ Identify word families that have a common cluster of letters representing a sound (e.g., tch).
- ☐ Discuss vocabulary relating to family relations (e.g., son, husband, father).
- ☐ Analyze different relationships in literature (e.g., *Romeo & Juliet*, *Huckleberry Finn*).

HISTORY
- ☐ Illustrate the hierarchical relationship in governments or governing bodies by using the genogram in this chapter.
- ☐ Discuss dynasties and royal families (e.g., the Ming dynasty, the Swazi royal family, European royalty).
- ☐ Outline the differences in relationships in democracy versus those in autocracies in which one person has power.

GEOGRAPHY
- ☐ Show how different by-products are derived from the parent source (e.g., diamonds and oil come from coal).
- ☐ Discuss relationships among countries in a commonwealth (e.g., the British commonwealth).

GENERAL SCIENCE
- ☐ Discuss the grouping of planets in the solar system and their relationship to the sun.
- ☐ Examine how animal systems differ in their relationships (e.g., ants in a colony, bees in a hive, doves mating for life).
- ☐ Show how through genetics you can predict chromosomal characteristics (e.g., blue eyes, twins).

MATH
- ☐ Show how a reciprocal relationship can be illustrated in math (e.g., $2 + 4 = 4 + 2$).
- ☐ Use a genealogical map to illustrate one-to-one and one-to-many correspondence.

FINE ARTS
- ☐ Design symbols to represent gender and relationships.
- ☐ Mix primary colors to show how a secondary color can be created (e.g., blue and red = purple).

SkyLight Training and Publishing Inc.

Family Relations

BRIDGING

In the Home — EVERYDAY ACTIVITIES IN THE HOME CAN BE USED TO TEACH THE SKILL OF **FAMILY RELATIONS**.

Invite children to dress up and act out family roles (e.g., big brother feeding baby sister; daughter showing daddy how to wash the dishes). Have them dress up accordingly and go through the motions of the activity.

Design your own family tree by cutting up photographs and pasting them on a chart to illustrate the relationships among family members.

Other occasions when family relationships can be mediated include
- playing a card game such as Rummy (grouping members of the same family of cards together)
- encouraging children to make greeting cards for family occasions (e.g., birthdays, weddings, and anniversaries)
- using puppet shows to work through attitudes toward new family members (e.g., a new baby or a new stepmother)

BRIDGING

In the Community

FAMILY RELATIONS CONCEPTUALIZES RELATIONSHIPS THROUGH USING KINSHIP AND THE GENOGRAM. IN A DISCUSSION OF VALUES IN COUNSELING SITUATIONS AND IN EXPLORING MULTICULTURAL RELATIONSHIPS, OTHER TYPES OR RELATIONS ALSO CAN BE EXAMINED IN THE AFFECTIVE MOTIVATIONAL AREAS AND DEVELOPED IN THE CREATIVE AREAS.

COUNSELING
- Develop an understanding of the roles and responsibilities of family members by examining the relationships between them.
- Examine institutions by identifying the roles and relationships of their members, discussing how changes in them can bring about improvement in interaction, functioning, achievement, and satisfaction

AFFECTIVE
Identify all the vertical and horizontal relationships you have with people in your daily life. Which relationships are close? Why?

Family Relations

BRIDGING

In the Community

CREATIVE

Relationships can be viewed in unusual and creative ways. Think of the variety of ways in which the relationships in the animal kingdom can be interpreted.

MULTICULTURAL

Develop an appreciation of different cultural structures by researching the family relationships that exist within each culture.

Cultural class . . .

For example, choose two cultures and examine relationships by use of a Venn diagram, as shown below:

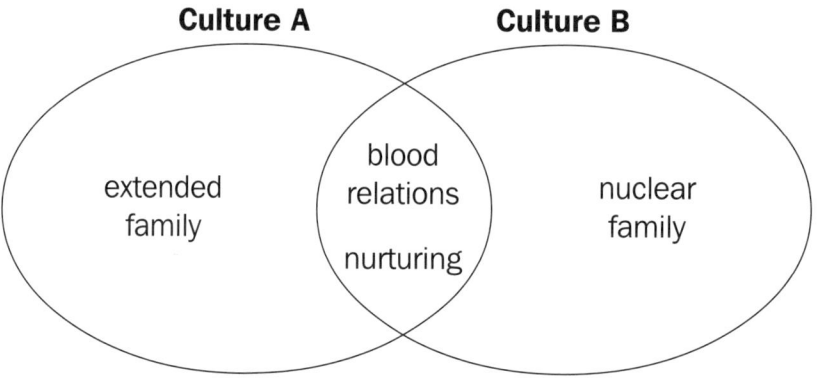

WORK PAGE

TRUE OR FALSE?

Give reasons for your answer.

1. An individual may have the same relationship with a number of different people, or he or she may have different relationships with a number of different people.

   _____
   _____
   _____
   _____

2. Family Relations uses kinship to illustrate that relationships are fixed and immutable, being based on the criteria that are used for their definition.

   _____
   _____
   _____
   _____

BRIDGING

A person's behavioral problems can be seen in terms of relationships and conflicts among family members. Evaluate the merits of changing a child's behavior by altering the patterns of interaction within the family.

_____
_____
_____
_____
_____
_____

SkyLight Training and Publishing Inc.

Family Relations

WORK PAGE

APPLICATION

Use this page to develop the ideas suggested in chapter 7.

CHAPTER 8

This instrument focuses on the cognitive operation of Temporal Relations, which means having an understanding of concepts of time.

Feuerstein's symbol for the instrument is a comparison of two aspects of time—natural time and "human-made" time.

Natural time is represented as day and night (moonlight or sunlight as seen through the window) and "human-made" time is represented by the clock (12 o'clock midnight and 12 o'clock noon). Both sources of information are needed to tell the time.

Temporal Relations

Temporal Relations

STRATEGY

Understanding Temporal Relations depends on the development and use of various cognitive functions.

For example, when working out a timetable for study, we need to understand how many hours are in a day and how many weeks are in a month (understanding of temporal concepts) *in order to work out what subject matter to study each day* (planning behavior) *and overcome the habit of procrastination* (blocking output response).

"Procrastination is the thief of time."
"Time is money."
"Time heals all wounds."
"How time flies."
"Do not squander time, for that is the stuff that life is made of."

Appreciating these quotations depends on the ability to understand concepts of time. Time is one of the most abstract concepts and can be described in a number of different ways—calendars (time as constructed by humans) or cycles of the moon (natural time). Managing time is one of the keys to effective living.

What Are Temporal Relations?

Understanding Temporal Relations means understanding concepts of time. For example, natural time includes the seasons of the year, the days and nights, rhythms of sleep, a heart beat, or a pulse. Natural time is approximate and relative. (For instance, during summer in Johannesburg in South Africa, night falls at about 8 p.m., whereas in Cape Town it is still daylight at 10 p.m. In contrast, time that is constructed by humans uses things such as clocks, calendars, and semesters. "Human-made" time is absolute and accurate (e.g., 1 hour = 60 seconds), but dependent on culture (e.g., the Jewish calendar year differs from both the Roman and Chinese calendars).

Why Are Temporal Relations Important?

- to appreciate how the past influences the present and how both past and present impact on the future
- to be able to plan ahead—work out short- and long-term goals
- to be able to follow a sequence of events from beginning to end
- to anticipate consequences of actions (e.g., what will happen next if I do this now?)
- to delay gratification (e.g., to restrain certain behavior until an appropriate time)

When and Where Do We Use Temporal Relations?

- in the home (e.g., routines of eating and sleeping)
- at school (e.g., following the school schedules or timetables and meeting deadlines)
- in the community (e.g., planning long-term projects)
- to function efficiently (e.g., planning ahead, learning from past experiences, following a sequence)

BRIDGING

In the School

NUMEROUS CLASSROOM EXPERIENCES CAN BE USED TO MEDIATE **TEMPORAL RELATIONS.** FOLLOWING ARE SOME EXAMPLES:

GENERAL
- ☐ Chart the birthdays of students in the class on a yearly planner (calendar).
- ☐ Motivate students to be responsible for returning library books on time.
- ☐ Draw up a school calendar depicting the events of the year (e.g., homecoming/football game, prom).

LANGUAGE ARTS
- ☐ Discuss proverbs related to time (e.g., "Time is money," "Procrastination is the thief of time.").
- ☐ Sequence stories and events in the correct chronological order.
- ☐ Examine the grammatical structure for indicating past, present, and future tenses (e.g., was, am, will be).

HISTORY
- ☐ Draw up time lines to illustrate different periods in history (e.g., Stone Age, Iron Age, etc.).
- ☐ Illustrate cause-and-effect situations in historical events (e.g., wars, revolutions, changes in government).

GEOGRAPHY
- ☐ Make different sundials to measure and record time by observing shadows.
- ☐ Explore the relationship between the position of the sun and earth in terms of the days and the seasons of the year.

GENERAL SCIENCE
- ☐ Illustrate life cycles in the animal kingdom to show the cyclical nature of metamorphosis (e.g., caterpillar, cocoon, butterfly).
- ☐ Solve problems of velocity using equations of time (e.g., time = distance/speed).

MATH
- ☐ Compare digital and analog time (e.g., 4:55 = five minutes to 5 o'clock).
- ☐ Use different devices to measure time (e.g., a burning candle and an egg timer).

FINE ARTS
- ☐ Explain the sequence and timing involved in printing processes (e.g., developing photographs or offset printing).
- ☐ Explore the relationship between time and artistic expression (e.g., in music or dance, etc.).

Temporal Relations

BRIDGING

In the Home

EVERYDAY ACTIVITIES IN THE HOME CAN BE USED TO TEACH THE CONCEPT OF **TEMPORAL RELATIONS**.

Design timetables for extracurricular activities in picture or graphic form, displaying them at home to remind children on which days they need to pack particular supplies to take to school.

Monday	⚽	(soccer)
Tuesday	🎨	(art)
Wednesday		
Thursday	🏊	(swimming)
Friday	🎤	(choir)

Make sundials or shadow sticks for the garden. Observe how the shade moves at different times of the day. Notice how the sizes of the different shadows change.

Other occasions when Temporal Relations can be mediated include
- ☐ developing an awareness of time by encouraging the use of watches, diaries or logs, and calendars
- ☐ teaching young children to organize their time (e.g., using the TV Guide to plan viewing time with suppertime and bathtime)
- ☐ making diaries or scrapbooks of holiday or vacation photos
- ☐ understanding/appreciating natural time (e.g., noting phases of the moon, changes in seasons, night and day)
- ☐ understanding "physiological" time (e.g., when our bodies tell us it's time to eat, sleep, etc.)

BRIDGING

In the Community

PERCEPTION OF CYCLES, RHYTHMS, AND TEMPORAL ORDER IN **TEMPORAL RELATIONS** CREATES AN AWARENESS OF LAWS THAT GOVERN THE SELF WITH VALUE IN COUNSELING AND EXPLORING AFFECTIVE DIMENSIONS. DIFFERENCES IN THESE TEMPORAL LAWS CAN BE HIGHLIGHTED IN CREATIVE TASKS AND EXPLORED IN MULTICULTURAL AREAS.

COUNSELING

Explore the concept of "personal time" in counseling.
- For example, in dealing with delinquent behavior, discuss how stealing something now consequently will lead to punishment later.

Help solve personal problems by analyzing whether a client is "in-step" or "out-of-step" with society.
- For example, is that individual living in the past or dwelling on the future?

AFFECTIVE

Gather personal photographs and place them on a time line.

Analyze how you have changed both physically and mentally over time.

Temporal Relations

BRIDGING

In the Community

CREATIVE
Temporal Relations can be used to promote creative thinking.

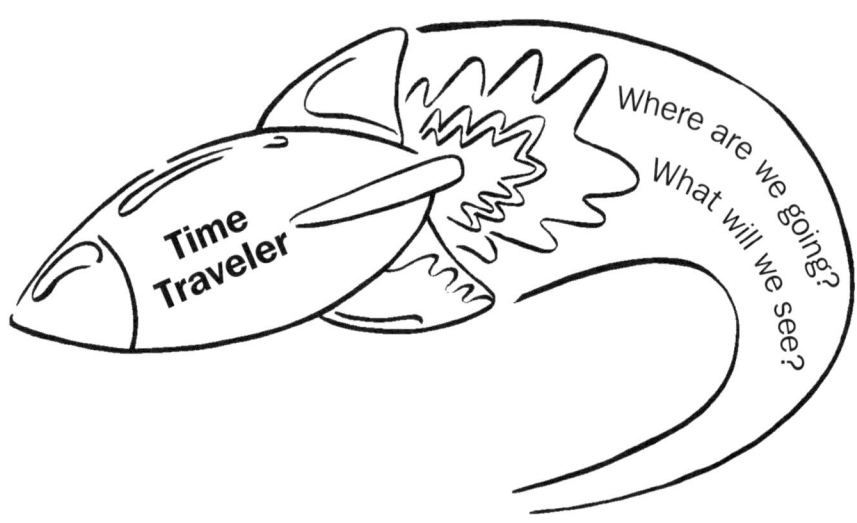

Imagine you are in a time machine and can travel through time, in effect turning the clock back or forward.

MULTICULTURAL
Temporal Relations can be used to promote empathy and appreciation of different cultures.

Cultural calendars . . .

Explore past, present, and future concepts in various cultures, for example
- the idea of reincarnation
- the concept of an afterlife
- the philosophy of life being of a circular nature as opposed to a linear one

WORK PAGE

TRUE OR FALSE?

Give reasons for your answer.

1. The perception of sequence and succession encourages the use of past and future to govern present activities.

   _____
   _____
   _____
   _____

2. Temporal orientation is based on relational thinking without which the child is confined to the "here and now."

   _____
   _____
   _____
   _____

BRIDGING

How can you use Mediated Learning Experiences (MLE) to teach the concept of time?

_____
_____
_____
_____
_____
_____
_____
_____

Temporal Relations

WORK PAGE

APPLICATION

Use this page to develop the ideas suggested in chapter 8.

CHAPTER 9

This instrument focuses on the cognitive operation of Orientation in Space II, where the cardinal compass points—north, south, east, and west—are taught. Feuerstein's symbol for this instrument is the compass rose, showing the points of N, NE, E, SE, S, SW, W, and NW. This symbol depicts the universal and absolute characteristic of using compass points when describing a position in space.

Orientation in Space II

Orientation in Space II

STRATEGY

Understanding Orientation in Space II depends on the development and use of various cognitive functions.

For example, to plot a journey we need to understand the absolute concerns of north, south, east, and west (understanding of spatial concepts), *plan the route systematically and logically* (need for planning behavior), *and work through each step on the map* (avoidance of trial-and-error output behavior).

Where are we on this map? In which direction must I travel to reach home? How can I give a precise and constant description of positions? Being able to answer these kinds of questions depends on having a good understanding of cardinal points (north, south, east, and west). This is what is described in Orientation in Space II.

In Orientation in Space I the terms *left, right, back* and *front* were introduced to show how objects relate to one another in space. Using this reference system, orientations are relative to individual positions (e.g., "If I turn around, then what is in front of me becomes what is behind me"). However, in Orientation in Space II, the points of the compass—north, south, east and west—are used. This reference system is absolute (e.g., North does not change if I turn around or change my position). The compass points are an objective, stable, and universally accepted manner of describing locations.

What Is Orientation in Space II?

Orientation in Space II teaches the skill of describing a position in space accurately by using the compass points of north, south, east, and west. This instrument involves recognizing that the system of compass-points reference is external and absolute (not dependent on the relative position of the referent), and that it is accurate, precise, and universal (a convention used throughout the world).

Why Is Orientation in Space II Important?

- to develop a system of reference to describe the position of objects in space accurately
- to appreciate that the compass points constitute a system of reference that is universal and absolute
- to use both the absolute, external system of compass points (north, south, east, and west) in conjunction with the relative, internal system (left, right, back, and front) when describing positions
- to bridge to areas where rules are absolute or fixed in problem solving

When and Where Do We Use Orientation in Space II?

- to describe the location of something precisely (e.g., a ship in distress needing to be rescued)
- to communicate directions (e.g., drawing maps as well as plotting trajectories or movements in space)
- to understand, from a psychological point of view, how orientation to things can change around a fixed point of view (e.g., a liberal point of view always being to the "left" of a conservative point of view; a pessimistic view always seeing the worst; with an optimistic view always seeing the best)

BRIDGING

In the School

NUMEROUS CLASSROOM EXPERIENCES CAN BE USED TO MEDIATE **ORIENTATION IN SPACE II.** FOLLOWING ARE SOME EXAMPLES:

GENERAL
- ☐ Draw patterns using a spirograph that has a fixed central point.
- ☐ Play Twister, Candy Land, or other board games using a compass-like dial with a spinning arrow that determines a fixed direction.
- ☐ Copy pictures using a grid and compass points as a guide.

LANGUAGE ARTS
- ☐ Create opportunities for pupils to direct one another along different routes using fixed landmarks as a reference.
- ☐ Use characters from literature as stimuli and invite students to give different perspectives (e.g., the Mad Hatter's view of reality in *Alice in Wonderland*).
- ☐ Talk fellow students through a maze by using compass points.

HISTORY
- ☐ Predict or speculate on past historical events that may repeat themselves in the future.
- ☐ Compare world maps of different periods and observe how boundaries have changed.
- ☐ Analyze war strategies used by famous generals.

GEOGRAPHY
- ☐ Explain how to use a compass and the difference between magnetic North and true North.
- ☐ Study how the earth is divided by imaginary lines of latitude and longitude.
- ☐ Find out about the rotations of the earth around the sun.
- ☐ Note how wind directions are named according to the direction from which they come (e.g., a westerly wind).

GENERAL SCIENCE
- ☐ Find animal habitats and plants that have a particular orientation for survival (e.g., migration of birds; sunflowers moving their heads to capture the sun's rays).
- ☐ Explain magnetic fields and their relation to the North Pole and South Pole.
- ☐ Explain the concept of gravity and how it affects our lives.

MATH
- ☐ Explain coordinate geometry by plotting x and y points on a graph.
- ☐ Draw angles of different degrees showing how 0 and 360 are North.
- ☐ Show how all geometry is based on lines moving from a fixed point.

FINE ARTS
- ☐ Design a building that takes into consideration the aesthetic and practical implications of the location (e.g., a north-facing house).
- ☐ Create mobiles, ensuring that objects balance around a fulcrum.

SkyLight Training and Publishing Inc.

Orientation in Space II

BRIDGING

In the Home

EVERYDAY ACTIVITIES IN THE HOME CAN BE USED TO TEACH THE CONCEPT OF **ORIENTATION IN SPACE II**.

Make a drawing of your house from different angle (e.g., from the northside and from the south side).

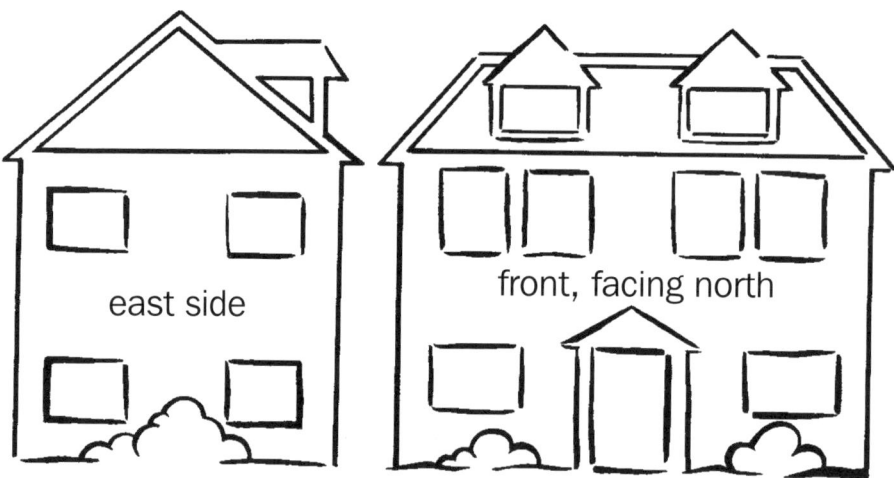

Follow a pattern or design, such as one for embroidery, by numbering squares on a grid.

Other occasions where Orientation in Space II can be mediated include
- planning an ideal kitchen, considering the fact that plumbing and electricity may need to remain in fixed positions
- drawing diagrams indicating where the important electrical switches are in your home
- setting up a sundial to show the direction of north
- planning a garden by selecting suitable shrubs for sun or shade to ensure optimum growth
- planning a family vacation using maps
- constructing a model following a grid plan

BRIDGING

In the Community

THE USE OF EXTERNAL, STABLE, AND ABSOLUTE SYSTEMS OF REFERENCE DESCRIBED IN **ORIENTATION IN SPACE II** IS VALUABLE IN SEEKING PERSPECTIVE DURING COUNSELING AS WELL AS IN THE ANALYSIS OF CULTURAL DIFFERENCES. SUCH REFERENTS CAN BE EXTENDED TO ANALYSIS OF THE SELF IN AN AFFECTIVE CAPACITY AS WELL AS BEING REPRESENTED IN UNUSUAL WAYS IN CREATIVE AREAS.

COUNSELING
- ☐ Discuss the concept of "rules of life" in counseling (i.e., the idea that certain laws that govern our lives are fixed and that we have to orientate our thinking to work within them).
- ☐ Encourage a problem-solving strategy whereby one works from fixed, known coordinates and explores solutions from this base.

AFFECTIVE

Explore the idea of "emotional coordinates" in terms of "Where do I place myself today in terms of happiness?"

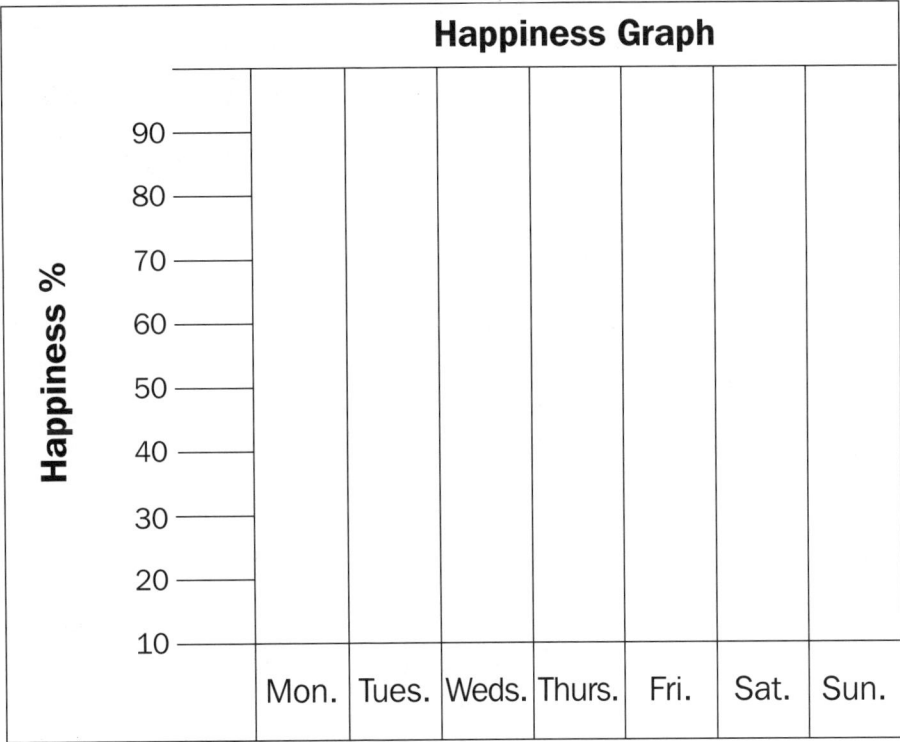

Show that although the emotional coordinate is fixed, the reasons for happiness are dynamic (e.g., Monday is a school day, on Wednesday a favorite sport is played, and Saturday is a day for going to the movies with friends).

Orientation in Space II

BRIDGING

In the Community

CREATIVE

Orientation in Space II can be bridged to many creative activities.

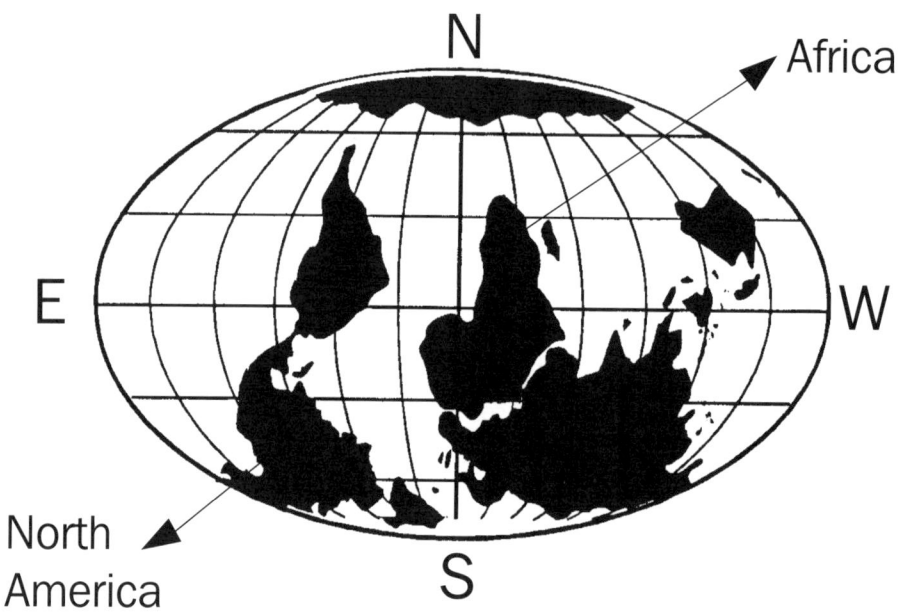

Explore the implications of our world upside down in space! North becomes south and east becomes west. How would plants, animals, and humans be affected?

MULTICULTURAL

Orientation in Space II can be used to highlight and appreciate the differences between cultures that exist in various continents of the world.

Cultural cardinal coordinates

Examine the great differences between
- Eastern and Western religions
- the way people dress in the Northern and Southern hemispheres
- Native tribes of Africa and of North America (How does their geographical orientation on earth relate to their cultural characteristics?)

WORK PAGE

TRUE OR FALSE?

Give reasons for your answer.

1. Orientation in Space II deals with the relative personal system of reference (i.e., the student's internal reference system regarding his or her orientations).

   _____
   _____
   _____
   _____

2. The fundamental tenet of absolute spatial reference is represented by cardinal compass points, coordinates, graphs, etc.

   _____
   _____
   _____
   _____

BRIDGING

Describe how the need for representation into areas other than space can be mediated to students, without losing sight of the value of an objective system of reference for communication.

_____
_____
_____
_____
_____
_____
_____

Orientation in Space II

WORK PAGE

APPLICATION

Use this page to develop the ideas suggested in chapter 9.

CHAPTER 10

This instrument focuses on the cognitive operation of Instructions, which involves *encoding* (giving) and *decoding* (receiving) information. Feuerstein's symbol for the Instructions is a diagram showing how an instruction involves an input phase (when the instruction is encoded), an elaboration phase (when the instruction is thought about), and an output phase (when the instruction is decoded and carried out). This instrument further illustrates how instructions can consist of either a single directive (e.g., do not walk on the grass) or a set of directions to follow (e.g., the steps in baking cookies).

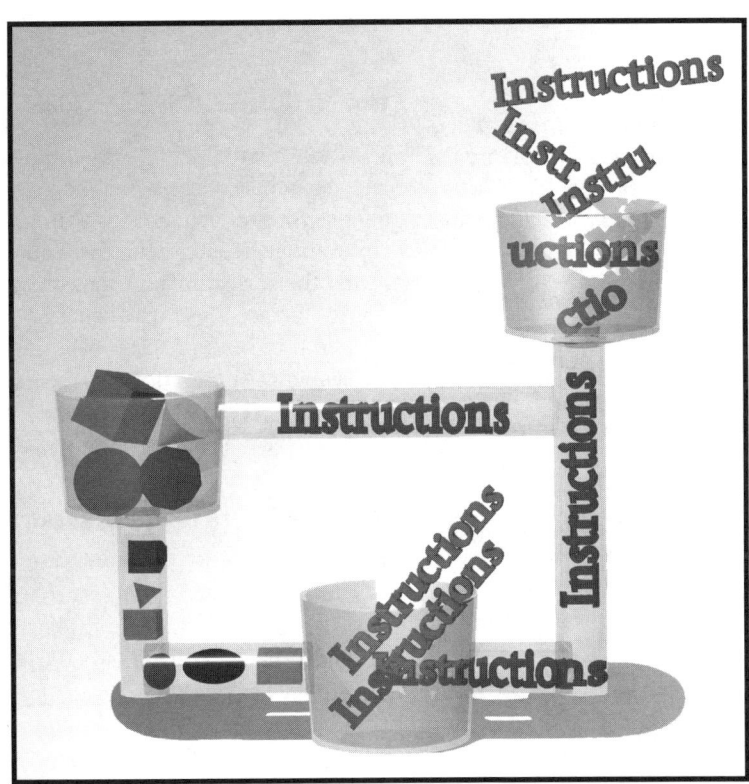

Instructions

Instructions

STRATEGY

Understanding Instructions depends on the development and use of various cognitive functions.

For example, when assembling a do-it-yourself table, we need to follow the directions given, such as what goes where and how (capacity to consider more than one source of information). *Furthermore, we need to think about what the final product will look like, proceed* (project virtual relations), *and be careful not to make any errors* (precise and accurate data output).

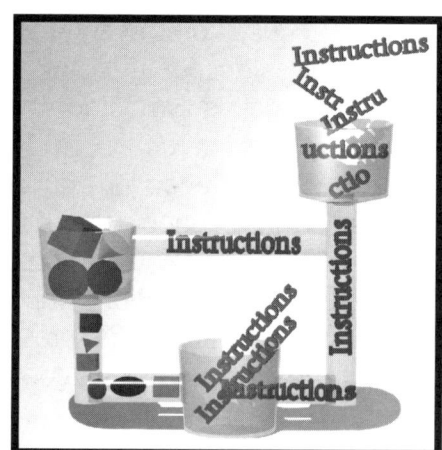

What dosage of medicine must I take? What questions must I answer in the exam? How do I fill out my federal tax return form? What are the rules of the game? The ability to answer these kinds of questions depends on having an ability to understand and follow instructions.

Understanding instructions involves both *encoding*—being able to give a command or a set of directions—as well as *decoding*—being able to translate what is meant by a command and carry it out, or to follow a set of directives. Instructions can be given and received in many different ways including auditory-verbal (directions given over the phone); written (a memo from the boss); visual (road signs or diagrams illustrating how to fix an appliance); and even nonverbally (interpreting a teacher's frown to mean "Come on now!").

What Are Instructions?

Instructions involve interpreting or giving a command, a message, or a set of directives or directions. Having a strategy helps with both encoding and decoding of instructions. A useful strategy is to ask the seven questions: Who? What? Why? When? How? Which? Where? Applying answers to these questions ensures that the correct sequence occurs in implementing the instructions. Errors in following instructions are also minimized if a strategy is followed.

Why Are Instructions Important?

The best way to illustrate the importance of being able to encode and decode instructions is to discuss the consequences of not giving or following instructions properly. For example, what are the consequences of a doctor not giving the correct instructions about dosage of medication? What are the consequences of not decoding (understanding) the essay topic on an exam? What are the consequences of not obeying the instructions of the road? Giving and receiving instructions is an integral part of our everyday life—at school, at home, and in the community.

When and Where Do We Use Instructions?

- We give and receive instructions at home from the moment we awake to the evening—from following the instructions on the oatmeal box to reading the instructions on how to operate the VCR at night.
- Our day at school is controlled through giving and following instructions: obeying the school rules, listening to the teacher's directions on how to conduct an experiment, telling someone where and when to pick us up.
- Our lives are regulated by instructions such as how to write a check, with whom to lodge a complaint, on what side of the road to drive.

BRIDGING

In the School

NUMEROUS CLASSROOM EXPERIENCES CAN BE USED TO MEDIATE **INSTRUCTIONS**. FOLLOWING ARE SOME EXAMPLES:

GENERAL
- ☐ Carefully analyze assignment topics and instructions on tests and exams to ensure that you structure the answers as specified.
- ☐ Follow the rules of a game to avoid conflict and confusion.
- ☐ Explain the procedure for checking out books from the library.
- ☐ Read instructions for operating computers or other appliances before using them.

LANGUAGE ARTS
- ☐ Apply spelling rules (e.g., *i* before *e* except after *c*).
- ☐ Stress the importance of following the instructions or stage directions indicated in a drama script (e.g., move to center stage).

HISTORY
- ☐ Discuss the protocol (e.g., parliamentary procedure) that everyone must follow during a session of Congress or during other governmental meetings.
- ☐ Investigate various laws that communities must abide by (e.g., civil laws).

GEOGRAPHY
- ☐ Follow directions to find a specific place on a map.
- ☐ Show the step-by-step procedure that manufacturers need to follow in the making of a product from raw materials (e.g., refining sugar from sugar cane).

GENERAL SCIENCE
- ☐ Emphasize the importance of following strict instructions and safety precautions when conducting a scientific experiment.
- ☐ Show how the dissection of plants involves following specific steps (e.g., in a flower dissection, starting from the sepals and working to the stigma).

MATH
- ☐ Explain how to decode story problems into mathematical operations.
- ☐ Demonstrate the importance of following mathematical rules (e.g., if you have brackets, multiple before you add).

FINE ARTS
- ☐ Show the sequence of processes involved in silk-screening or making batik.
- ☐ Research a dance such as the waltz or the Macarena, then write or diagram the instructions for that dance.

SkyLight Training and Publishing Inc.

Instructions

BRIDGING

In the Home

EVERYDAY ACTIVITIES IN THE HOME CAN BE USED TO TEACH **INSTRUCTIONS.**

Build a model airplane by following the instructions carefully. Make sure you use all the correct airplane parts in the correct places and that you assemble it in the correct order—otherwise, the finished product might be unsuccessful.

Construct a tree house or play house from ready-cut pieces of timber. Follow instructions to make sure it is safe and correctly assembled.

Other occasions when instructions can be mediated include
- ☐ growing plants from seedlings
- ☐ following the rules of a game
- ☐ operating and fixing new appliances
- ☐ writing an invitation
- ☐ taking telephone messages
- ☐ baking a cake
- ☐ setting the table

BRIDGING

In the Community

THE OPERATIONS OF ENCODING AND DECODING FOCUSED ON IN THE **INSTRUCTIONS** INSTRUMENT ARE CRITICAL TO PROBLEM SOLVING DURING COUNSELING AND PLAY A SIGNIFICANT ROLE IN INTERPRETING MULTICULTURAL CODES OF BEHAVIOR. SUCH OPERATIONS CAN BE EXTENDED TO THE EFFECTIVE AND CREATIVE AREAS WHERE THEIR TRUE VALUE CAN BE EXPLORED IN DIVERSE WAYS.

COUNSELING

- ☐ Mediate "coping with life" strategies through following instructions (e.g., a pragmatic approach to using pay telephones and parking meters, reading schedules or timetables, filling in forms, interpreting traffic signs).
- ☐ Demonstrate the need for decoding or encoding during career counseling (e.g., following your employer's memos, interpreting blueprints or plans, and working through business correspondence handbooks).

AFFECTIVE

Examine the "emotional" component of instructions in the home by exploring how messages are communicated and interpreted both verbally and nonverbally.

Instructions need not be written. They can be transmitted in many different ways ranging from a verbal statement to a sign or gesture, a symbol, or even a body stance. Such cues cause an emotional reaction.

SkyLight Training and Publishing Inc.

Instructions

BRIDGING

In the Community

CREATIVE

The concept of Instructions can be used as a stimulus for creative, diverse, individualistic, and "reverse" thought wherein sequence and laws of order are purposefully tampered with.

- Imagine the steps of your dad's favorite chocolate cake recipe have been mixed in the instructions pot.
- Imagine pulling out each step at random and follow the recipe no matter what order it is in.
- What does your cake look like?

MULTICULTURAL

The Instructions instrument can be used as a springboard to examine protocol and procedure in diverse cultures.

Cultural codes of conduct...

Discuss and contrast the rituals that various cultures practice such as the following:

- wedding ceremonies
- baptism (Christian tradition), bar mitzvah or bas mitzvah (Jewish tradition), quinceañera (Mexican tradition), etc.
- food, eating, personal cleanliness
- prayer, spiritualism, and life instructions from a higher order/a supreme being, etc.

Highlight the strict adherence that is enforced in certain cultures in regard to order and carrying out of instructions. Discuss the negative consequences when codes of conduct are broken.

WORK PAGE

TRUE OR FALSE?

Give reasons for your answer.

1. The "mediationally deprived" individual cannot carry out complex instructions because he or she is unable to identify and integrate the separate elements in the input and elaboration phase.

   _____
   _____
   _____
   _____

2. When using the Instructions instrument, written instructions are encoded in the input phase, processed in the elaboration phase, and expressed in the output phase.

   _____
   _____
   _____
   _____

BRIDGING

Teachers often comment that students start to work even before the instructions for the task are completely given and explained. What cognitive deficiencies have to be overcome in such situations and how can you improve a student's ability to perceive and carry out instructions correctly?

_____
_____
_____
_____
_____
_____

SkyLight Training and Publishing Inc.

Instructions

WORK PAGE

APPLICATION

Use this page to develop the ideas suggested in chapter 10.

CHAPTER 11

The Numerical Progressions instrument deals with the cognitive operations involved in looking for rules that explain the relationship between events. These rules are then applied in order to anticipate and predict new events. Feuerstein's symbol for this instrument is a succession of circles and triangles. The rules that govern this particular progression is that a circle follows a triangle, the triangles stay the same, and the circles change in size and fill in. One can predict possible continuation of this progression based on this rule.

Numerical Progressions

Numerical Progressions

STRATEGY

Understanding Numerical Progressions depends on the development and use of various cognitive functions.

For example, when predicting when the next leap year will be, we need to understand the passage of time (temporal concepts), work out the four-year intervals (project virtual relationships), and calculate accurately (precise and accurate data output).

If the color of the traffic light is now red, what will be the color that it changes to? In knitting a scarf according to a pattern, I have just knitted a purl stitch—what will the next stitch be? If I see a flash of lightning now, what can I expect to hear very soon? If it is September now, what will next month be?

Being able to answer these kinds of questions depends on having a good understanding of progressions. This means understanding that there are laws and rules that govern events, and that the future can be predicted based on knowledge of the past. It involves inducing the rule (thunder always follows lightning) and deducing the event from the rule (if I see lightning, I should hear thunder soon).

What Are Numerical Progressions?

Progressions are recurring sequences or successions of events that are governed by a rule or formula. When the rule is discovered, new situations can be anticipated based on that rule.

Numerical Progressions are a progression that involves the modality of number (i.e., a recurring set of numbers based on a rule such as 3, 6, 9 . . . being multiples of 3, etc.).

Why Are Numerical Progressions Important?

- to understand the relationships between events and distinguish between chance events (which are unpredictable) and causality (concerning events that we can predict based on a rule or hypothesis generated from past occurrences).
- to be able to identify different types of progressions (e.g., cyclical—as in the seasons of the year—and linear—as in the chapters of a book).
- to appreciate ascending (adding on) and descending (subtracting) progressions (e.g., eating more calories than one burns up results in weight gain—ascending progression; spending more money than one earns in bankruptcy—descending progression).
- to distinguish between finite (e.g., the life cycle of a silkworm) and infinite progressions (e.g., patterns of evolution).

When and Where Do We Use Numerical Progressions?

- to discover the rules governing repeated patterns of behavior (e.g., in dancing a waltz, one moves in a sequence of three steps).
- whenever we need to predict what will happen in the future (e.g., working out the exponential growth in population of the planet).

BRIDGING

In the School

NUMEROUS CLASSROOM EXPERIENCES CAN BE USED TO MEDIATE **NUMERICAL PROGRESSIONS.** FOLLOWING ARE SOME EXAMPLES:

GENERAL
- ☐ Explain how block scheduling of courses can be integrated so students know where to go and what books to pack on any given day.
- ☐ Show how the acquisition of skill and knowledge is a prerequisite for progression from one standard to the next.

LANGUAGE ARTS
- ☐ Play auditory memory games (e.g., "I went to the store and bought a …" in which each child repeats the progression and adds on one item.).
- ☐ Identify the rhyme and rhythm within poetry, and then create your own poem using repeated rhyme and rhythm.

HISTORY
- ☐ Study the sequence of historical events in order to predict what may occur in the future (e.g., events leading to the outbreak of war).
- ☐ Show how demographics predict future outcomes based on past occurrences (e.g., spread of AIDS, etc.).

GEOGRAPHY
- ☐ Look at examples of how one can predict the effect of an accumulation of repeated occurrences (e.g., exposure to small amounts of radiation can eventually kill).
- ☐ Consider cycles in which events reoccur in the same sequence continuously (e.g., phase of the moon, months of the year, changes of tides, times of day).

GENERAL SCIENCE
- ☐ Show how progressions occur in nature (e.g., water cycles, blood circulation, biorhythms).
- ☐ Research how human immune systems are built upon by repeated doses of vitamin C over regular periods of time.
- ☐ Discuss natural rhythms of animals (e.g., birds migrating, fish spawning, mating cycles).

MATH
- ☐ Isolate the source of error in progressions by tracing the process step by step, tracing the process backwards, checking that you are using the correct formula.
- ☐ Examine progressions in mathematics and how they are represented graphically (e.g., ascending, descending, or linear graphs).

FINE ARTS
- ☐ Print repeated patterns for fabric design.
- ☐ Show how an illusion of depth can be created in a drawing by using the rules of perspective (e.g., repeatedly shrinking an image).
- ☐ Explore the rhythms of music and song to identify the underlying beat.

SkyLight Training and Publishing Inc.

Numerical Progressions

BRIDGING

In the Home

EVERYDAY ACTIVITIES IN THE HOME CAN BE USED TO TEACH **NUMERICAL PROGRESSIONS**.

Movement and music games can be played by building up a sequence of claps and steps based on a particularly rhythm (e.g., stand, crouch, cross your legs and up again—(repeat)—stand, crouch, cross your legs . . .)

Design and knit a sweater by repeating certain stitches to create a particular design (e.g., rib = 1 purl stitch and 1 plain stitch repeated, stocking stitch = 1 row plain and 1 row purl, etc.).

Other occasions when Numerical Progressions can be mediated include
- threading beads to create a pattern for a necklace
- using numbered and/or multicolored building blocks, Brio Mec, or Lego toys to create a sequence
- designing and installing a mosaic or tile floor in the home
- generating rules to determine the daily routine in the home (e.g., wake-up time, bed time, reading time, bath time)

In the Community

BRIDGING

THE PRINCIPLE OF DISCOVERING RULES OR LAWS THAT GOVERN SUCCESSFUL EVENTS CAN BE APPLIED IN THE AREAS OF COUNSELING AND COMMUNITY WORK WHEN STRUCTURING OF FUTURE EVENTS AND FORECASTING IS IMPORTANT. IT ALSO HAS VALUE IN THE AFFECTIVE AREA FOR PERSONAL RESTRUCTURING OF ROUTINES. FOR INSTANCE, LAWS, RHYTHMS AND RECURRENT PHENOMENA HOLD GREAT IMPORTANCE IN DIFFERENT CULTURES AND CAN BE USED IN DIVERSE WAYS TO PROMOTE CREATIVITY.

COUNSELING

- Demonstrate the need to look for connections between events to establish their cause and effect in order to handle future problems (e.g., what was the sequence or pattern of events leading up to a family feud).
- Illustrate the importance of rituals, traditions, and laws governing communities and explain how they lead to stability and regulation (e.g., the tradition of going to church every Sunday, Sabbath meal each Friday, a family reunion).

AFFECTIVE

Encourage introspection of personal constants, rhythms, and progressions in behavior by looking at the past, present, and future (e.g., *happy* remains constant and *silly* progresses to serious and confident).

The idea of being "master of one's own destiny" can be a powerful tool in affective or emotional areas. Students can be empowered by being able to understand laws of the universe and how they affect them.

Numerical Progressions

BRIDGING

In the Community

CREATIVE

The principle of Numerical Progressions can be used as a stimulus for many creative ideas whereby outcomes change because laws and rules have to be altered.

Think about it:
How would the world be if the pattern of aging was reversed in plants and animals? We would be born old men and women and become smart and wise children or babies!!!

MULTICULTURAL

Numerical Progressions can be used as a stimulus for discussion of the importance of rhythms, cycles, and patterns of behavior in the preservation and transmission of culture.

Cultural constants and continuities
- Research patterns of festivals, fasting, and other observances in various cultures (e.g., Jewish, Mexican, Indian, Chinese, Native American, African-American, etc.).
- Contrast annual cycles of Eastern and Western cultures based upon spiritual philosophies and religions.
- Consider at the importance placed on rhythm in many of the Eastern ways of life for physical as well as mental endeavors (e.g., yoga, karate, mantras in meditation).

WORK PAGE

TRUE OR FALSE?

Give reasons for your answer.

1. Numerical Progressions demonstrate how a rule can be extracted by looking at the relationships between two elements.

2. Discovery of a law or rule and its application allows us to predict, with a fair degree of accuracy, future events.

BRIDGING

The fundamental tenet of Numerical Progressions is the discovery of a rule that can be applied to predict outcomes in new or different successive events. The mediationally deprived child will think things happen by accident rather than because of specific determinants. How do we reconcile the two? Is there a place for fate, luck, or accident in this?

Numerical Progressions

WORK PAGE

APPLICATION

Use this page to develop the ideas suggested in chapter 11.

CHAPTER 12

The Transitive Relations instrument deals with the cognitive operations of transferring information we have from two pairs of items to a third pair. Feuerstein's symbol for this instrument is a person solving a problem that has been encoded in symbols. The person takes in information (B is less than A, B is equal to C, A is not equal to C, and A is greater than B); thinks through the problem (what is the relationship between A and C?); and, by transferring information, expresses the solution (A is greater than C and C is equal to B).

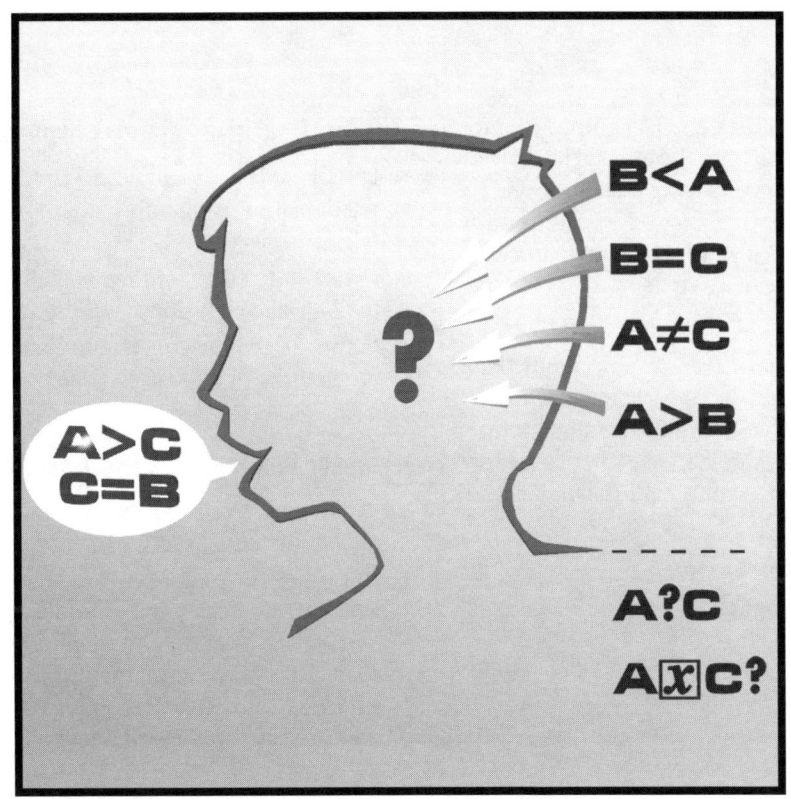

Transitive Relations

Transitive Relations

STRATEGY

Understanding Transitive Relations depends on the development and use of various cognitive functions.

For example, when deciding on the fastest mode of transport to use, one has to gather information about all the options (capacity to consider more than one source of information), *rank them in terms of speed* (comparative behavior and logical evidence), *and transfer the information from one source to the other* (worked through output response).

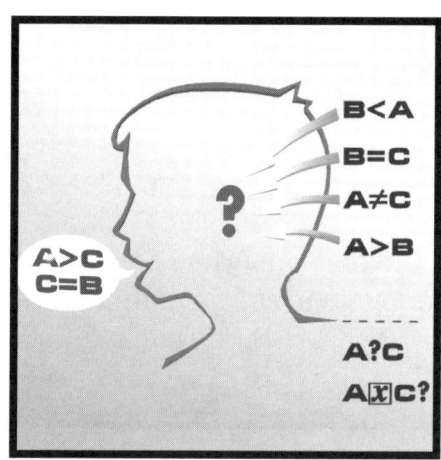

If Mark runs faster than Gina and Gina runs faster than Sam, will Sam beat Mark into the athletic team? How old is Jane if she is two years older than Mary and Mary is three years younger than Sue, who is 10? If car A, is more expensive than car B, which is the same price as car C, do we know the price of car A?

Being able to answer these kinds of questions depends on being able to solve problems of Transitive Relations. This means finding the conclusion by transferring information from two premises. It involves using the common term in both statements (Gina is slower than Mark but faster than Sam) to reach a conclusion about a third statement (Mark is faster than Sam).

What Are Transitive Relations?

Transitive Relations refers to the "transitivity of relationship." If information is given about two statements, then a conclusion can be inferred about a third statement by transferring the relationship of the common term. For example, if we know the relationship between A and B and between B and C, then we can transfer the information to reach a conclusion about A and C. The Transitive Relations Instrument uses the following symbols:

- $>$ = greater than and $<$ = less than
- $=$ (equal to) and $\neq$ (not equal to)
- x = impossible to know, need to solve

Why Are Transitive Relations Important?

- to make inferences and draw conclusions about relationships using information from other relationships
- to test statements for their validity—so as not to jump to illogical conclusions
- to move from the concrete to abstract by solving problems with the use of symbols ($>$, $<$, x, and $=$)

When and Where Do We Use Transitive Relations?

- to discover the relationships between sets of items (e.g., in ranking best to worst, or tallest to shortest, etc.)
- wherever we need to make inferences from the implications of the given information (e.g., if we are given the cost of one brand of margarine as being more than another brand, we still do not have enough information to draw conclusions about a third brand)

BRIDGING

In the Classroom

NUMEROUS CLASSROOM EXPERIENCES CAN BE USED TO MEDIATE **TRANSITIVE RELATIONS.** FOLLOWING ARE SOME EXAMPLES:

GENERAL
- ☐ Rank reading books in order of difficulty.
- ☐ Design a chart in order to match the level of skill of players in a tennis tournament.
- ☐ Arrange class members in height order for a photograph.
- ☐ Compare situations involving "jumping to conclusions" versus those when we have sufficient information.

LANGUAGE ARTS
- ☐ Develop vocabulary to describe characteristics of objects or a range of feelings through using a continuum of words (e.g., happy, excited, elated).
- ☐ Show how synonyms are equal and antonyms are not equal (e.g., happy = glad; thick ≠ think).

HISTORY
- ☐ Rank nations in terms of economic and political power.
- ☐ Develop a realistic understanding of perceptions and attitudes by discussing different points of view and ranking them from extreme to moderate.

GEOGRAPHY
- ☐ Measure and record temperatures over a period of time to indicate which areas are hotter than others.
- ☐ Rank planets according to their distance from the sun.

GENERAL SCIENCE
- ☐ Discuss ranking of elements in the periodic table in terms of relationships by asking if hydrogen is less dense than oxygen and oxygen is less dense than helium, then which is less dense—hydrogen or helium?
- ☐ Research and chart the gestation period for various animals.
- ☐ Rank animals in terms of the number of offspring and look for reasons (e.g., mammals reproduce less than insects).

MATH
- ☐ Use the > and < sign to illustrate relationships (e.g., to illustrate a larger or smaller quantity or number of elements in a set).
- ☐ Use the ≠ sign to describe a relationship in which the elements are different.
- ☐ Show how x is used to illustrate the unknown in algebraic formula.

FINE ARTS
- ☐ Select your top ten songs and rank them from best to worst.
- ☐ Estimate the hue or value of a color depending upon the colors that have been mixed.

Transitive Relations

BRIDGING

In the Home

EVERYDAY ACTIVITIES IN THE HOME CAN BE USED TO MEDIATE **TRANSITIVE RELATIONS.**

Settle family disputes by encouraging siblings to rank themselves according to age. Explain why older children get different privileges (e.g., Jennifer > Paul > Mary, therefore Jennifer goes to bed later than Paul and Mary).

Explain to children that in order to solve a problem you need to consider all the relevant information. For example, Martha is shorter than John. Mary is 3 feet tall. How tall is John? Is it possible to solve this problem without having more information?

Other occasions or purposes when Transitive Relations can be mediated:
- [ ] to help alleviate exam stress by ranking study material in terms of volume and priority, and drawing up a study timetable
- [ ] to read labels on foodstuffs and rank according to fat or sugar content
- [ ] to rank music for a party or disco (e.g., favorite songs first)
- [ ] to rank household chores in an order to ensure they are completed on a timely basis

BRIDGING

In the Community

THE IDEA OF LOOKING FOR DIFFERENCES BETWEEN ELEMENTS IN ORDER TO RANK THEM IN **TRANSITIVE RELATIONS** CAN BE TRANSFERRED TO THE PRINCIPLE OF PRIORITIZING IN COUNSELING AND COMMUNITY WORK. IT ALSO HELPS US SOLVE PROBLEMS IN THE AFFECTIVE AND MULTICULTURAL AREAS. THE USE OF SIGNS AND SYMBOLS TO DENOTE THIS ORDERING CAN BE EXTENDED TO CREATIVE AREAS WHERE DISORDER CAN ALSO BE EXPLORED.

COUNSELING

Demonstrate the importance of ranking community issues in order of their degree of urgency for resolutions.
- This in turn can help in the planning of future community projects.

Use the idea of ranking to illustrate "weighing the alternatives."
- This idea is useful in the formulations of strategies to solve problems in business and the community as it can save a great deal of time and expense.

AFFECTIVE

Children can be shown at any early age how to prioritize things they want or need. This in turn helps them make decisions and mediates the concept of delaying gratification.

By ranking the importance of acquiring a toy, the child can make a decision on how to spend his or her pocket money.

Transitive Relations

BRIDGING

In the Community

CREATIVE

The principle of using the signs >, <, =, and ≠ to order or rank elements can be explored in absurdity in creative thinking.

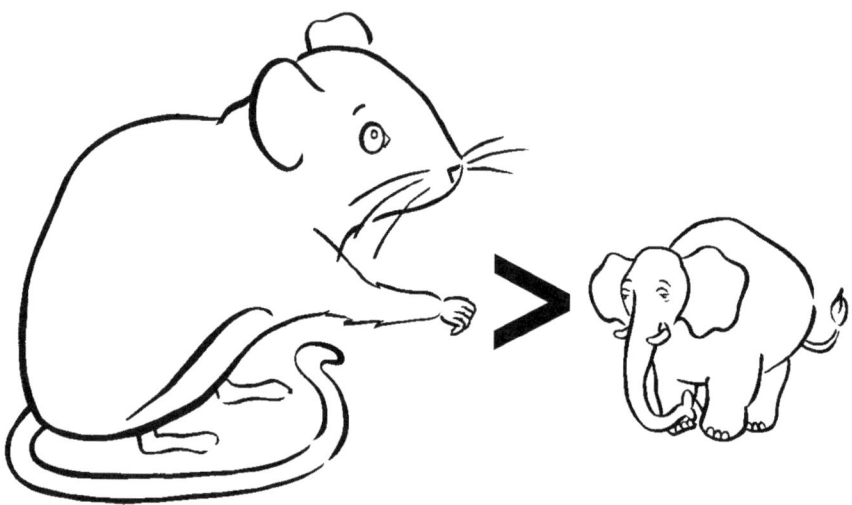

Make the above statement true without changing the sign or the elements around. Brainstorm in what ways an elephant could be smaller than a mouse.

MULTICULTURAL

The idea of equality, inequality, and ranking has deep roots in various cultures. These concepts often form the basis of harmony and conflict in intercultural groups, as well as within the particular mainstream/predominant culture.

Cultural congruencies

Contrast cultural groups in terms of what is considered equal or unequal, greater or less than, as in the following:
- males/females
- young/old
- polygamy/monogamy
- federal law/religious law
- public secular education/religious education

WORK PAGE

TRUE OR FALSE?

Give reasons for your answer.

1. Ordering or ranking elements in Transitive Relations must be done on a specific dimension to establish hierarchy (e.g., size, shape, importance).

   _____
   _____
   _____
   _____

2. In Transitive Relations, information regarding the relative order between a set of elements can be transferred to other elements about which no information is given.

   _____
   _____
   _____
   _____

BRIDGING

To what extent does the order of elements, events, and people affect our perceptions of their hierarchy or importance? For example, consider the following situations
- reading a list of children's names aloud
- viewing the credits run before a movie
- attaching numbers 1, 2, 3, 4, . . . to objects or ideas

How can we avoid assumptions and perceptions based on hierarchy in a classroom situation?

_____
_____
_____
_____

Transitive Relations

WORK PAGE

APPLICATION

Use this page to develop the ideas suggested in chapter 12.

CHAPTER 13

The Syllogisms instrument focuses on the cognitive operations involved in syllogistic reasoning, where from two given premises that have a common middle term, a third premise is deduced—called the conclusion. For example, "All men die, Socrates is a man, therefore Socrates will die."

Syllogisms involve understanding sets and set membership, and the symbol that Feuerstein uses for the instrument is a series of overlapping circles that represent sets. Some members belong to more than one set, which is indicated by a subset and intersecting sets.

Syllogisms

Syllogisms

STRATEGY

Understanding Syllogisms depends on the development and use of various cognitive functions.

For example, in order not to be seduced by advertisements for products endorsed by famous people, one first has to make the link between the person and the product (consider more than one source of information), *and then identify the logical error that buying the product will lead automatically to being included in the same subset as the famous person* (inferential-hypothetical thinking) *so as* not *to buy impulsively* (appropriate output behavior).

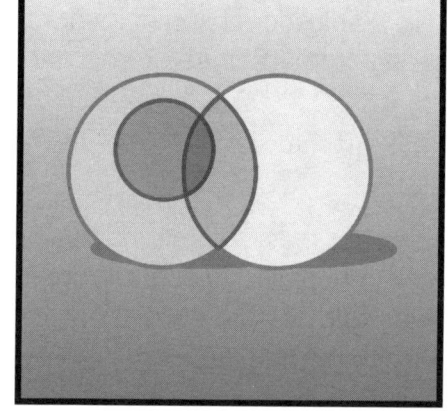

If the age restriction of a film is over twenty-one, can a ten-year-old attend? Is the statement "All fat people are happy" correct?

The ability to answer these kinds of questions depends on the ability to understand sets and subsets and to reason syllogistically. To answer the age-restriction question involves understanding mutually exclusive sets. The film is for all members of a set of people over twenty-one. If you belong to a set of people younger than twenty-one, then you are excluded from the rules governing the over–twenty-one set. Answering the second question about generalizations involves identifying sets and subsets. *Happy* is a description of a subset of the universal set of fat people and thus cannot be used to describe the universal set because there are some fat people who are not happy.

What Are Syllogisms?

Syllogisms are a form of reasoning with a simple construction. From two related assumptions comes a conclusion that is logically valid but need not necessarily be true. For example, the syllogism "All men are hostile, Adam is a man, therefore Adam is hostile" is logically valid but incorrect because the first premise is a generalization that is untrue.

Syllogisms are based on the following four identical kinds of relationships between sets:

- identical sets—where ALL x are y, and ALL y are x
- exclusive sets—where NO x are y, and NO y are x
- subsets of universal sets—where ALL x are y, and SOME y are x
- intersecting sets—where SOME x are y, and SOME y and x

Why Are Syllogisms Important?

- to understand and critically interpret statements made about the relationships between things in everyday life
- to detect incorrect conclusions based on untrue statements
- to reason logically

When and Where Do We Use Syllogisms?

- to understand rules and regulations at home, at school, and in the community
- to interpret news items in the media
- to appreciate humor, understand advertisements, and note errors in logic

BRIDGING

In the School

NUMEROUS CLASSROOM EXPERIENCES CAN BE USED TO MEDIATE **SYLLOGISMS.** FOLLOWING ARE SOME EXAMPLES:

GENERAL
- Show how cognition can be seen as the intersecting set of all subjects as thinking skills are common to all disciplines.
- Draw a Venn diagram to illustrate class participation in common extramural activities.

LANGUAGE ARTS
- Analyze literature in terms of mutually exclusive sets according to the style or period in which the selection was written.
- Study advertisements or commercials by interpreting the slogans and identifying the logic used to convince consumers.
- Identify the parts of speech used in language and categorize these by sets (e.g., common nouns are a subset of nouns).

HISTORY
- Identify the humor in political or editorial cartoons by analyzing the syllogistic portrayal of a given situation.
- Arrange artifacts into mutually exclusive sets from different historical periods (e.g., the Stone Age or the Iron Age).

GEOGRAPHY
- Show how the same temperature expressed in Fahrenheit and Celsius constitutes two identical sets.
- Explore the various subsets within the universal set of citizenship (e.g., in terms of origin, American citizens can be German, Dutch, Chinese, Mexican, and so on).

GENERAL SCIENCE
- Explain how omnivores make up the intersecting set of herbivores and carnivores.
- Use sets and subsets to illustrate classification of plants and animals (e.g., reptiles are a subset of animals).

MATH
- Use Venn diagrams to teach the mathematical symbols (e.g., $\cup$ = universal set, $\cap$ = intersecting set.
- Generate different examples for identifying sets (e.g., all even numbers and all numbers divisible by two constitute identical sets).

FINE ARTS
- Explain how an orchestra is made up of a number of subsets that play together in unison.
- Appreciate different forms of dance by identifying the overlaps (e.g., modern dance is a combination of jazz and other dance forms).

SkyLight Training and Publishing Inc.

Syllogisms

BRIDGING

In the Home

EVERYDAY ACTIVITIES IN THE HOME CAN BE USED TO MEDIATE **SYLLOGISMS**.

Teach children the logic of syllogisms by applying it to the rules of the home. (For instance, all children under 12 must be in bed by 8 o'clock. Mark is under 12, therefore he must be in bed by 8 o'clock.)

Discourage stereotyping when assigning household chores (e.g., washing dishes and washing the car should not be exclusively boys' or girls' jobs).

Other occasions when Syllogisms can be mediated include
- detecting the "odd one out" by applying rules for membership of a set (for example, a hammer does not belong in a silverware drawer in the kitchen)
- using intersecting sets to find common interests for family entertainment
- explaining to young children that the family name is the intersecting set, but they retain their own identity in their first name

In the Community

BRIDGING

SYLLOGISTIC THINKING CAN BE USED EFFECTIVELY IN THE CRITICAL ANALYSIS OF PROPOSITIONS AND PREMISES PRESENTED IN THE AREAS OF COUNSELING, PROMOTING A NEED FOR CONSIDERING THE IMPLICATIONS OF GIVEN PROPOSITIONS, AND LOOKING FOR LOGICAL EVIDENCE IN MULTICULTURAL FIELDS. THE DANGERS OF OVERGENERALIZATION AND STEREOTYPING FROM MISUSE OF **SYLLOGISMS** HAVE THEIR IMPORTANCE IN THE AFFECTIVE AND CAN PROVIDE STIMULI FOR CREATIVE EXPLORATION OF ILLOGICAL REASONING.

COUNSELING

- ☐ Use the overlapping sets theory in syllogisms to aid students in career choice (e.g., show how different professions have common elements (mathematical ability), and similar professions may call for different skills).
- ☐ Demonstrate the importance of formal propositional logic in overcoming prejudice, overgeneralizations, and stereotyping (e.g., all short people have inferiority complexes, all kids are naughty) that wrongly transfer the characteristics of the subset to the universal set.

AFFECTIVE

Evaluations of feelings relating to being a member of different sets is important in developing the socio-emotional side of the student (e.g., show children how they can use Venn diagrams to illustrate social circles and sets):

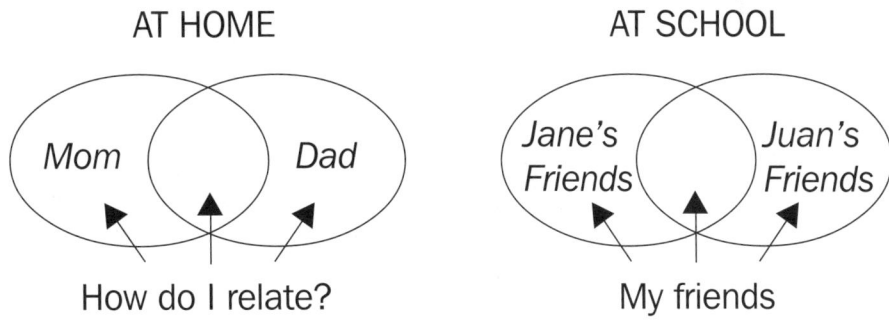

Encourage students to analyze feelings which may be common to many social groups or unique to one specific group.

Syllogisms

BRIDGING

In the Community

CREATIVE

Use the principle of illogical, verbal reasoning in the creative mode to illustrate the importance of valid versus invalid conclusions:

All monkeys are hairy.
My daddy is hairy.
Therefore, my daddy is a monkey!

MULTICULTURAL

Examining how cultures overlap in language, laws, customs and so on helps us to understand and look for the roots of their acceptance as part of a particular culture.

Cultural collectivism

Examine cultures in terms of their joint ownership of certain laws, customs, and rituals and, at the same time, identify their mutual exclusivity.

For example, consider
- the belief in many Eastern cultures that the spirit proceeds to a higher plane after death
- various coming-of-age rituals, religious or otherwise, in different cultures

WORK PAGE

TRUE OR FALSE?

Give reasons for your answer.

1. Syllogisms are based entirely on deductive inference involving the application of a generalization or rule to a variety of stimuli.

   _____
   _____
   _____
   _____

2. The ability of a child to make inferences in Syllogisms stems from a difficulty in projecting virtual relationships.

   _____
   _____
   _____
   _____

BRIDGING

Feuerstein wrote, "There are hidden dangers in using syllogisms that are based on stereotypes or overgeneralizations." What are these hidden dangers and how does one avoid them when working with children?

_____
_____
_____
_____
_____
_____
_____

Syllogisms

WORK PAGE

APPLICATION

Use this page to develop the ideas suggested in chapter 13.

CHAPTER 14

The Representational Stencil Design instrument focuses on the cognitive operations involved in mentally reconstructing an event or a design by looking at the end product. Feuerstein's symbol for this instrument is a series of templates of different shapes and colors that can be used to create a prescribed design when superimposed, one on top of each other, in a particular order.

Representational Stencil Design

Representational Stencil Design

STRATEGY

Understanding Representational Stencil Design depends on the development and use of various cognitive functions.

For example, we can mentally solve problems concerning atoms even though we cannot see them by selecting the relevant information (systematic exploration and interiorization), *generating and applying rules* (inferential hypothetical thinking), *and detecting and avoiding errors* (worked through output response).

W hy has this cake flopped? Where have I left my keys? Who was the killer in the murder mystery and how was the murder done?

The ability to answer these kinds of questions depends on the ability to think inferentially and hypothetically. This means that we must be able to reconstruct events in the sequence in which they occurred, with the help of available cues, and test out hypotheses against available evidence. One must mentally retrace one's steps to establish where the keys were left or go through the process of baking the cake to work out which part of the recipe went wrong. Solving a murder mystery means testing out different hypotheses one has against the available evidence. As new evidence comes to the fore, it changes our understanding of the previous information.

What Is Representational Stencil Design (RSD)?

RSD involves mentally working out which stencils are used and in which order to create a particular design. This process of discovering which stencils are "hidden" behind a design is the same mental process used in discovering the meaning hidden in an event or discovering the motives underlying a particular action. For example, "acting out" or "disruptive" behavior in children could mask a cognitive dysfunction. One would need to unravel the layers and look at available cues to test out this hypothesis.

Why Is RSD Important?

- to appreciate that our senses can be tricked by illusions and that "seeing is not always believing" (e.g., the earth moves, not the sun)
- to distinguish between what we see and what we know (e.g., the earth looks flat, but when we reconstruct all the knowledge that we have about the earth we know that it has to be round)
- to unravel hidden meanings behind events (e.g., reconstructing a murder to solve the crime)
- to look for hidden agendas (e.g., propaganda)

When and Where Do We Use RSD?

- in the home (e.g., gaining insight into why the water in the swimming pool turned green)
- at school (e.g., gaining insight into the group dynamics of the class)
- in the community (e.g., understanding that some services were discontinued in order for others to be financed)
- to function creatively and efficiently (e.g., problem solving or looking for scientific reasoning)

BRIDGING

In the School

NUMEROUS CLASSROOM EXPERIENCES CAN BE USED TO MEDIATE **REPRESENTATIONAL STENCIL DESIGN.** FOLLOWING ARE SOME EXAMPLES:

GENERAL
- ☐ Construct plans to facilitate changes in the curriculum of schools in transition.
- ☐ Consider all factors that contribute to stress in schools and devise strategies for minimizing the stress.

LANGUAGE ARTS
- ☐ Analyze poetry to identify the author's intention and appreciate the hidden meanings.
- ☐ Encourage critical reflection of essays to check whether thoughts are clearly and accurately communicated.

HISTORY
- ☐ Facilitate understanding of events by considering the historical perspectives (e.g., events leading up to a coup d'etat).
- ☐ Trace the historical revolution or path of inventions (e.g., the wheel).

GEOGRAPHY
- ☐ Research geographical phenomena to substantiate the reality (e.g., the earth is round, not flat).
- ☐ Decode meteorological charts to predict and report on the weather conditions.

GENERAL SCIENCE
- ☐ Retrace steps to determine what went wrong in a science experiment.
- ☐ Research the cause of strange phenomenon (e.g., asking Why do whales beach themselves? Why aren't the silkworms spinning?).

MATH
- ☐ Check a complex mathematical problem to find the error.
- ☐ Describe how geometric shapes have been constructed (e.g., two equilateral triangles make a square).
- ☐ Reconstruct numbers by using different operations and numerals (e.g., 24 can be constructed either by 6×4 or $12 + 12$).

FINE ARTS
- ☐ Explain the procedure in making ceramics.
- ☐ Teach music appreciation by identifying overlap of various instruments used in a composition.
- ☐ Identify elements of representational art versus other types of art forms (e.g., abstract or performance art).

SkyLight Training and Publishing Inc.

Representational Stencil Design

BRIDGING

In the Home

EVERYDAY ACTIVITIES IN THE HOME CAN BE USED TO MEDIATE **REPRESENTATIONAL STENCIL DESIGN.**

Children often confuse what they know and what they perceive in reality—what they cannot see often just does not exist for them. They do not, for example, accept there are baby birds hidden in a nest they can see, even though there are sounds emanating from it.

Teach children that some things exist even though they cannot be seen (e.g., explain that harmful germs and bacteria, although invisible to the naked eye, lead to tooth decay).

Other occasions when RSD can be mediated include
- describing the steps followed in constructing a Lego or Brio Mec tower or building (e.g., with Legos, start with a red flat base block).
- explaining the idea of intellectual realism (e.g., a tree has roots; people exist on the other side of the world)
- assisting young children dressing for a special occasion by deciding which clothes they are going to wear and sorting out the order in which to put them on
- describing how to reconstruct a geometric design using a spirograph
- guiding children toward understanding that there are a set of circumstances or reasons behind behavior of family members (e.g., "brother is angry because . . .")

In the Community

BRIDGING

THE CONCEPT OF MENTALLY RECONSTRUCTING A WHOLE WITH THE HELP OF AVAILABLE CUES IN RSD HAS GREAT SIGNIFICANCE IN THE ANALYSIS OF PERSONAL AND FAMILY PROBLEMS IN COUNSELING AND EXPLORATION OF MANIFEST BEHAVIOR IN AFFECTIVE AREAS. IT CAN ALSO BE TRANSFERRED TO THE PHENOMENON OF PERCEPTUAL INFERENCES THAT CAUSE US TO LOOK AT MULTICULTURAL ACTIVITIES AND RITUALS FAR MORE ANALYTICALLY. IN CREATIVE AREAS, ONE CAN EXPLORE A FURTHER CONCEPT OF RSD—NAMELY, INTELLECTUAL REALISM AND WHAT IS HIDDEN, BUT KNOWN TO BE THERE.

COUNSELING

Illustrate the importance of looking at available cues to gain insight into a child who has learning disabilities.

☐ This helps us to deduce causes and remediate the problem.

Use the idea of reconstructing or "looking back" to establish the specific order of circumstances that led up to an event/happening in the community, such as

☐ strikes by a union of mine workers

☐ a rapid increase of homeless people in a central business district

Extend the concept of mental reconstruction to the solving of crimes, looking for missing persons, examining the reasons for company mergers, and analyzing bull or bear runs in the stock market.

Representational Stencil Design

BRIDGING

In the Community

AFFECTIVE

The cognitive tasks of perception, inferential thinking, and logical deduction found in RSD can be bridged to everyday-life examples the child may encounter.

Children need to be guided into identifying hidden dangers by looking for cues and projecting possible outcomes—ideally avoiding dangerous situations.

BRIDGING

In the Community

CREATIVE
Use the principles of superimposition and mental manipulation of stencils to stimulate creative thought. A group of individuals can come up with surprising results.

For instance, students can create their own "unreal" animal using stencils. Their classmates can be challenged to work out the order of parts of real animals that made it up.

MULTICULTURAL
The fundamental of understanding the end result, by mentally seeking the structures upon which it is built, bridges well into multicultural areas where we need to comprehend traits and customs rather than take them at face value.

Representational Stencil Design

BRIDGING

In the Community

Cultural cues and clues

Explore behaviors in different cultures that deliver a "hidden message" which can be misconstrued. Consider the following examples:

- The custom of burping loudly after a meal in the Middle East is a compliment, but can be misread by Westerners.
- The averting of eyes in many cultures contradicts the Western importance of eye contact in communication.

Look for cues and clues to trace back the manifestation of expressions, traditions, and customs in certain cultures, such as

- the "evil eye"—Middle East
- saving face—Far East
- kow-towing—China
- Day of the Dead celebration—Mexico
- Mardi Gras—Western Europe

WORK PAGE

TRUE OR FALSE?

Give reasons for your answer.

1. Representational Stencil Design consists of tasks in which the student must construct a design through motor manipulation of pieces that will match the model in the end result.

   _____
   _____
   _____
   _____

2. Because perceptual reality is never really reversable, the order in which events are perceived makes no great difference in determining the outcome.

   _____
   _____
   _____
   _____

BRIDGING

How would you mediate the notion of hidden agendas, such as those in propaganda, to children?

_____
_____
_____
_____
_____
_____

Representational Stencil Design

WORK PAGE

APPLICATION

Use this page to develop the ideas suggested in chapter 14.

REPRESENTATIONAL STENCIL DESIGN CAN BE SEEN AS A SYNTHESIS OF INSTRUMENTS 1–13.

1.	*Organization of Dots* involves identifying unique characteristics of stimuli and projecting relationships. In RSD you need to identify the characteristics of each stencil and organize them in order to reconstruct the design.	**Organization of Dots**
2.	*Comparison* involves identifying similarities and differences between stimuli according to relevant criteria. In RSD you need to compare stencils according to the criteria of color and shape in order to reconstruct the design.	**Comparisons**
3, 4.	*Orientation in Space* involves identifying directionality. In RSD you need to determine the orientation of each stencil in order to reconstruct the design.	**Orientation in Space I & II**
5.	*Analytic Perception* involves identyifying the parts that make up the whole. In RSD you need to analyze which stencils can be synthesized into the reconstructed whole.	**Analytic Perception**
6.	*Categorization* involves grouping according to like characteristics. In RSD you need to group the stencils according to color and shape in order to select the correct stencil from the group.	**Categorization**
7.	*Illustrations* involves finding solutions to problems. In RSD the solution is not always obvious and one has to think divergently or indirectly in order to reconstruct the design.	**Illustrations**

SkyLight Training and Publishing Inc.

REPRESENTATIONAL STENCIL DESIGN CAN BE SEEN AS A SYNTHESIS OF INSTRUMENTS 1–13.

8. *Family Relations* involves describing connections between people according to a given formula. In RSD you need to describe the connections between stencils according to a given formula.	**Family Relations**	
9. *Temporal Relations* involves understanding the order of events. In RSD you need to sequence the stencils correctly in order to reconstruct the design.	**Temporal Relations**	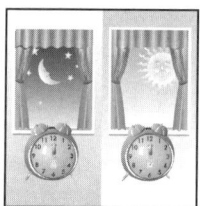
10. *Instructions* involves following a set of rules or procedures. In RSD you need to reconstruct the design according to certain rules.	**Instructions**	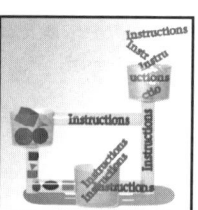
11. *Numerical Progressions* involves predicting an outcome based on a formula. In RSD you need to predict the outcome of a design by mentally superimposing the stencils in a given sequence.	**Numerical Progressions**	
12. *Transitive Relations* involves making inferences in order to rank items. Is RSD we need to rank the size and shape of stencils in order to establish the seqence of the final design.	**Transitive Relations**	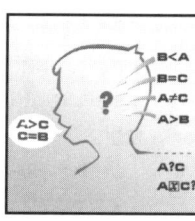
13. *Syllogisms* involves making deductions. In RSD you need to deduce the final design based on previously established premises.	**Syllogisms**	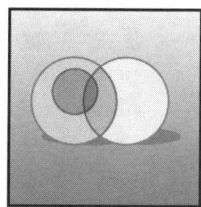

Appendix 1

Answers to Work Pages (True/False Questions)

Chapter 1
1. True
2. True

Chapter 2
1. True
2. False
   Comparison involves looking at differences as well as similarities.

Chapter 3
1. True
2. True

Chapter 4
1. False
   Analytic Perception involves a synthesis activity also, as well as examination of elements and their relationships.
2. True

Chapter 5
1. True
2. False
   Through induction the rule is discovered, and then applied by deduction in categorization.

Chapter 6
1. True
2. False
   Without sequencing or linking of the events, the meaning, humor, or absurdity of situations in Illustrations is missed.

Chapter 7
1. True
2. False
   Family Relations is the one Instrument that shows relationships as flexible phenomena that will change according to criteria for their definition.

Chapter 8
1. False
   Sequence and succession encourages the use of past and present to govern future activities.
2. True

Chapter 9
1. False
   Orientation in Space II uses external, stable, and absolute systems of reference.
2. True

Chapter 10
1. True
2. False
   Written instructions have to be decoded by the learner by elaborating and encoding verbally.

Chapter 11
1. False
   A rule for a progression can only be established if it pertains to more than two elements.
2. True

Chapter 12
1. True
2. True

Chapter 13
1. False
   Syllogisms also involve induction that requires generalization of a rule from a number of specific instances.
2. True

Chapter 14
1. False
   The student must use mental manipulation to reconstruct designs.
2. True

SkyLight Training and Publishing Inc.

Appendix 2

10 Criteria of Mediated Learning Experience (MLE)

1. **Intentionality and Reciprocity**
   Mediation is a mutual interaction. The mediator has the intention to share and the learner wants to receive.

2. **Meaning**
   Mediation of meaning means enthusiastically sharing your aims. It answers the learner's questions as to why the activity is important.

3. **Transcendence**
   Transcendence is bridging from the immediate experience to underlying principles and related activities and ideas.

4. **Competence**
   Mediation of competence means instilling in the mediatee a positive belief in his/her ability to succeed.

5. **Self-Regulation and Control of Behavior**
   Self-regulation and control of behavior involve "thinking about your own thinking" and adapting your responses.

6. **Sharing**
   Sharing promotes sensitivity to others and emphasizes working together.

7. **Individuation**
   Individuation is the acknowledgment and appreciation of uniqueness and independence.

8. **Goal Planning**
   Goal planning is the process whereby the mediatee is guided to set, plan, and achieve goals.

9. **Novelty and Challenge**
   Challenge is the feeling of excitement and determination when confronting a new and difficult task.

10. **Self-Change**
    Self-change is the recognition, acceptance, and monitoring of continual changes that occur within oneself.

Appendix 3

Lists of Cognitive Functions and Dysfunctions

	Input	
1.	Clear	Blurred and sweeping
	Perception	
2.	Systematic	Impulsive
	Exploration of a learning situation	
3.	Precise and accurate	Impaired
	Receptive verbal tools and voncepts	
4.	Well-developed	Impaired
	Understanding of spatial concepts	
5.	Well-developed	Impaired
	Understanding of temporal concepts	
6.	Well-developed	Impaired
	Ability to conserve constancies	
7.	Precise and accurate	Impaired
	Data gathering	
8.	Well-developed	Impaired
	Capacity to consider more than one source of information.	

SkyLight Training and Publishing Inc.

Output

1.	Mature	Egocentric
	Communication modalities	
2.	Participatory	Blocking
	Output responses	
3.	Worked through	Trial-and-error
	Output responses	
4.	Adequate	Impaired
	Expressive verbal tools	
5.	Precise and accurate	Impaired
	Data output	
6.	Accurate	Impaired
	Visual transport	
7.	Appropriate	Impulsive/Acting-out
	Behavior	

Elaboration

1.	Accurate	Inaccurate
	Definition of the problem	

2.	Ability to	Impaired ability to
	Select relevant cues	

3.	Ability to	Inability to
	Engage in spontaneous comparative behavior	

4.	Broad and wide	Narrow and limited
	Mental field	

5.	Need for	Impaired need for
	Spontaneous summative behavior	

6.	Ability to	Inability to
	Project Virtual Relationships	

7.	Need for	Lack of need for
	Logical evidence	

8.	Ability to	Inability to
	Internalize events	

9.	Ability to use	Impaired
	Inferential-hypothetical thinking	

10.	Ability to use	Impaired
	Strategies for hypothesis testing	

11.	Need for	Lack of
	Planning behavior	

12.	Adequate	Impaired
	Elaboration of cognitive categories	

13.	Meaningful	Episodic
	Grasp of reality	

About the Cognitive Research Program Manual Team

Mervyn Skuy

Mervyn Skuy is Professor and Head of the Division of Specialized Education at the University of the Witwatersrand in South Africa. He has a Ph.D. in psychology and is a clinical and educational psychologist. As the founder and director of the Cognitive Research Program at the University, he has initiated and led numerous research, training, and community projects in Feuerstein's approaches, including the Learning Potential Assessment Device, Instrumental Enrichment, and Mediated Learning Experience. He has taught and conducted research in these approaches in South Africa as well as in the U.S., Canada, and Israel.

Reuven Feuerstein

Reuven Feuerstein, Ph.D., professor and researcher, is an eminent cognitive psychologist whose groundbreaking research and practice in cognitive learning and mediation is established in more than seventy countries. He developed the Instrumental Enrichment program and the Learning Propensity Assessment Device and is the director of the International Center for the Enhancement of Learning Potential Hadassah-WIZO-Canada Research Institute in Israel. The collaboration between Prof. Feuerstein and Prof. Skuy commenced when the latter spent a year with Prof. Feuerstein in Israel studying and researching his approaches. Feuerstein's theories and approaches are considered to be of great relevance to the evolving multicultural society in South Africa.

Mandia Mentis

Mandia Mentis, an educational psychologist, works in the areas of teacher training, life-skills education, and cognitive research. She coordinated numerous projects of the Cognitive Research Program, implementing Feuerstein's Instrumental Enrichment, Mediated Learning Experience, and Learning Potential Assessment Device in remedial, counseling, pastoral, school, parenting, and teacher-training contexts. She holds a master's degree in educational psychology and recently immigrated to New Zealand, where she lectures in the Department of Teaching and Learning and helps to run the program of educational psychology at Massey University.

Marilyn Dunn

Marilyn Dunn-Bernstein is an eminent educator with nearly thirty years experience in all types of educational environments. She holds a Ph.D. and Master's Degree in Education as well as a degree in Human Behavior. With both a research and practical background, her special interest is in the celebration of diversity in learning, and the development of the individual's creative potential. For ten years, she worked in the Cognitive Research Unit at the University of the Witwatersrand, developing materials used in Feuerstein's Instrumental Enrichment and Mediated Learning programs. She has applied these programs to enhance the learning of gifted disadvantaged students.

Marilyn is currently in Australia where she is an educational consultant to various schools. She conducts teacher-student workshops in the development of cognitive and creative thinking skills and lectures in Feuerstein methodology. Also, she develops thinking skills materials for Australian and New Zealand students.

Fleur Durbach

Fleur Durbach has been involved in remedial education for eighteen years. She has worked as a researcher in the Cognitive Research Program, and has applied Feuerstein's Instrumental Enrichment and Mediated Learning Experience extensively in the areas of remedial and preschool education, as well as in parenting skills. She is currently working in a preparatory school where she is a member of the assessment team and the remedial committee, and is completing her B. Ed. degree in remedial education.

Marténe Mentis

Marténe Mentis has worked in the areas of education, business, and desktop publishing. She has worked as a researcher with the Cognitive Research Program, and has applied Feuerstein's Instrumental Enrichment and Mediated Learning Experience in secondary and tertiary educational settings. In addition, she implemented a research project using Feuerstein's program in a small mining town in South Africa. She holds a degree in Fine Art and a master's degree in education. She recently immigrated to New Zealand, where she helps to run workshops on Mediated Learning Experience.

Bibliography

Burden, R. L. 1990. Whither research on Instrumental Enrichment? Some suggestions for future action. *International Journal of Cognitive Education and Mediated Learning* 1(1): 83–86. (Now called *Journal of Cognitive Education.*)

Feuerstein, R. 1979. *The dynamic assessment of retarded performers.* Baltimore, MD: University Park Press.

Feuerstein, R., and Feuerstein, S. 1991. Mediated Learning Experience: A Theoretical Review. In *Mediated Learning Experience (MLE): Theoretical, psychosocial and learning implications,* edited by R. Feuerstein, P. S. Klein, and A. J. Tannenbaum, 3–52. London: Freund Publishing House.

Feuerstein, R. and Jensen, M. 1980. Instrumental Enrichment: Theoretical basis, goals and instruments. *Educational Forum* 44 (4): 401–23.

Feuerstein, R., Rand, Y., and Hoffman, M. 1979. *The dynamic assessment of retarded performers, the learning potential assessment device, theory instruments and techniques.* Baltimore, MD: University Park Press.

Feuerstein, R., Rand, Y., Hoffman, M. and Miller, R. 1980. *Instrumental Enrichment: An intervention program for cognitive modifiability.* Baltimore, MD: University Park Press.

Greenberg, K. H. 1990. Mediated learning in the classroom. *International Journal of Cognitive Education and Mediated Learning* 1 (1): 63–71.

Kozulin, A. 1990. Mediation: Psychological activity and psychological tools. *International Journal of Cognitive Education and Mediated Learning* 1 (2): 151–59.

Kozulin, A. (Ed.). 1997. *The ontogeny of cognitive modifiability: Applied aspects of Mediated Learning Experience and Instrumental Enrichment.* Jerusalem: ICELP.

Presseisen, B., and Kozulin, A. 1994. Mediated learning: The contributions of Vygotsky and Feuerstein in theory and practice. In *On Feuerstein's Instrumental Enrichment: A Collection,* edited by M. Ben-Hur, 51–82. Palatine, IL: IRI/Skylight Publishing, Inc.

Presseisen, B., Smey-Richman, B., and Beyer, F. S. 1994. Cognitive development through radical change: Restructuring classroom environments for students at risk. In *On Feuerstein's Instrumental Enrichment: A Collection,* edited by M. Ben-Hur, 193–260. Palatine, IL: IRI/Skylight Publishing, Inc.

Sharron, H. 1987. *Changing children's minds: Feuerstein's revolution in the teaching of intelligence.* London: Souvenir Press.

Skuy, M. (Ed.). 1996. *Mediated Learning Experience in and out of the classroom*. Arlington Heights, IL: IRI/SkyLight Training and Publishing, Inc.

———. 1997. Crosscultural and interdimensional implications of Feuerstein's construct of Mediated Learning Experience. *School Psychology International* 18, 119–135.

Skuy, M. et al. 1990. Combining Instrumental Enrichment and creativity/socioemotional development for disadvantaged gifted adolescents in Soweto, Part 1. *International Journal of Cognitive Education and Mediated Learning* 1 (1): 25–31.

———. 1990. Combining Instrumental Enrichment and creativity/socioemotional development for disadvantaged gifted adolescents in Soweto, Part 2. *International Journal of Cognitive Education and Mediated Learning* 1 (2): 93–102.

Skuy, M., Goldstein, I., Mentis, M., and Fridjhon, P. 1998. A cognitive approach to promoting multicultural awareness and co-existence in the classroom. *Journal of Cognitive Education* (in press).

Skuy, M., Lomofsky, L., Green, L., and Fridjhon, P. 1993. Effectiveness of Instrumental Enrichment for pre-service teachers in a disadvantaged South African community. *International Journal of Cogitive Education and Mediated Learning* 3 (2): 92–108.

Skuy, M., and Mentis, M. 1992. Applications and adaptations of Feuerstein's Instrumental Enrichment program among the disadvantaged population in South Africa. In *Cognition and Educational Practice: An International Perspective Volume I (Part B)*, edited by J. Carlson, 105–27. Greenwich, CT: JAI Press.

Skuy, M., Mentis, M, Durbach, F., Cockcroft, K., Fridjhon, P., and Mentis, M. 1995. Crosscultural comparison of effects of Instrumental Enrichment on children in a South African mining town. *School Psychology International* 16, 265–282.

Tzuriel, D., and Alfassi, M. 1994. Cognitive and motivational modifiability as a function of the Instrumental Enrichment (IE) program. *Special Services in the Schools* 8 (2): 91–128.

Index

Affective development
    Analytic Perception in, 29
    Comparisons in, 13
    Family Relations in, 53
    Illustrations in, 45
    Instructions in, 37, 77
    Numerical Progressions in, 85
    Organization in, 5
    Orientation in Space I in, 21,
    Orientation in Space II, 69
    Representational Stencil Design in, 110
    Syllogisms in, 101
    Temporal Relations in, 61
    Transitive Relations in, 93
Alphabetical order, 2
Analysis, 25
    applications of, 26
    definition of, 26
    importance of, 26
Analytic Perception, 25–32
    Representational Stencil Design in, 114
    teaching in the community, 29–30
    teaching in the home, 28
    teaching in the school, 27

Behavior, self-regulation and control to, 118
Blanket of emotions, 29
Body language, 77
Brainstorming, 94

Cardinal compass points, 66
Cartoons, application of, in multicultural learning, 46
Categorization, 33–40
    application of, 34
    definition of, 34
    importance of, 34
    Representational Stencil Design in, 115
    teaching in community, 37–38
    teaching in home, 36
    teaching in school, 35
Cause-and-effect
    Illustrations in, 45
    problem solving in, 42, 45
    Temporal Relations in, 59

Challenge, 118
Checklists, 4
Chronological order, 59
Cognitive functions, ix
Cognitive functions and dysfunctions, 119–121
Community
    teaching Analytic Perception in, 29–30
    teaching Comparisons in, 13–14
    teaching Family Relations in, 53–54
    teaching Instructions in, 77–78
    teaching Numerical Progressions in, 85–86
    teaching Organization in, 5–6
    teaching Orientation in Space I in, 21–22
    teaching Orientation in Space II, 69–70
    teaching problem solving in, 45–46
    teaching Representational Stencil Design in, 109–111
    teaching Syllogisms in, 100–102
    teaching Temporal Relations in, 61–62
    teaching Transitive Relations in, 93–94
Comparisons, 9–16
    applications of, 10
    definition of, 10
    importance of, 10
    Representational Stencil Design in, 115
    teaching in the community, 13–14
    teaching in the home, 12
    teaching in the school, 11
Comparison table, 14
Competence, 118
Conflict resolution, 21
Cooperation, as means of problem solving, 44
Counseling
    Analytic Perception in, 29
    Categorization in, 37
    Comparisons in, 13
    Family Relations in, 53
    Illustrations in, 45
    Instructions in, 77
    Numerical Progressions in, 85
    Organization in, 5
    Orientation in Space I in, 21
    Orientation in Space II, 69
    Syllogisms in, 101

    Temporal Relations in, 61
    Transitive Relations in, 93
Creative activities
    Analytic Perception in, 30
    Categorization in, 37
    Comparisons in enhancing, 14
    in developing organizational skills, 6
    family relationships in, 54
    Illustrations in, 46
    Instructions in, 78
    Numerical Progressions in, 86
    Organization of Dots in, 6
    Orientation in Space I in, 22
    Orientation in Space II, 70
    Representational Stencil Design in, 111
    Syllogisms in, 102
    Temporal Relations in, 62
    Transitive Relations in, 94
Cultural calendars, 62
Cultural treasure chest, 14

Decision making
    Analytic Perception in, 29
    Comparisons in, 13
    Organization of Dots in, 5
Decoding, 73, 74
Disorganization, 5
Disorientation, 19

Elaboration, 121
Encoding, 73, 74
Episodic grasp of reality, 2

Family Relations, 49–56
    applications of, 50
    definition of, 50
    importance of, 50
    Representational Stencil Design and, 116
    teaching in the community, 53–54
    teaching in the home, 52
    teaching in the schools, 51
    family therapy, 21
Family tree, 52
Feelie wheel, 13
Feeling collage, 13
Feuerstein, Reuven, 2, ix
Fine arts
    Categorization in, 35
    Comparisons in, 11
    family relationships in, 51
    Instructions in, 75
    Numerical Progressions in, 83
    Organization of Dots in, 3
    Orientation in Space I in, 19
    Orientation in Space II, 67

    problem solving in, 43
    Representational Stencil Design in, 107
    Syllogisms in, 99
    Temporal Relations in, 59
    Transitive Relations in, 91
General science
    Categorization in, 35
    Comparisons in, 11
    family relationships in, 51
    Instructions in, 75
    Numerical Progressions in, 83
    Organization of Dots in, 3
    Orientation in Space I in, 19
    Orientation in Space II, 67
    problem solving in, 43
    Representational Stencil Design in, 107
    Syllogisms in, 99
    Temporal Relations in, 59
    Transitive Relations in, 91
Genogram, 53
Geography
    Categorization in, 35
    Comparisons in, 11
    family relationships in, 51
    Instructions in, 75
    Numerical Progressions in, 83
    Organization of Dots in, 3
    Orientation in Space I in, 19
    Orientation in Space II, 67
    problem solving in, 43
    Representational Stencil Design in, 107
    Syllogisms in, 99
    Temporal Relations in, 59
    Transitive Relations in, 91
Goal planning, 118

History
    Categorization in, 35
    Comparisons in, 11
    family relationships in, 51
    Instructions in, 75
    Numerical Progressions in, 83
    Organization of Dots in, 3
    Orientation in Space I in, 19
    Orientation in Space II, 67
    problem solving in, 43
    Representational Stencil Design in, 107
    Syllogisms in, 99
    Temporal Relations in, 59
    Transitive Relations in, 91
Home
    teaching Analytic Perception in, 28
    teaching Comparisons in, 12
    teaching Instructions in, 76
    teaching Numerical Progressions in, 84

teaching Organization of Dots in, 4
teaching Orientation in Space I in, 20
teaching Orientation in Space II, 68
teaching problem solving in, 44
teaching Representational Stencil Design in, 108
teaching Syllogisms in, 100
teaching Temporal Relations in, 60
teaching Transitive Relations in, 92
Horizontal relationships, 53
Human-made time, 57, 58
Illustrations, 41–48
    Representational Stencil Design in, 114
Individuation, 118
Input, 120
Instructions, 73–80
    application of, 74
    definition of, 74
    importance of, 74
    Representational Stencil Design in, 116
    teaching in the community, 77–78
    teaching in the home, 76
    teaching in the schools, 75
Intentionality, 118
Interpersonal development
    comparison in promoting, 13
    organization in promoting, 5

Kinship, 53

Language arts
    Categorization in, 35
    Comparisons in, 11
    family relationships in, 51
    Instructions in, 75
    Numerical Progressions in, 83
    Organization of Dots in, 3
    Orientation in Space I in, 19
    Orientation in Space II, 67
    problem solving in, 43
    Representational Stencil Design in, 107
    Syllogisms in, 99
    Temporal Relations in, 59
    Transitive Relations in, 91
Lateral thinking, 46

Math
    Categorization in, 35
    Comparisons in, 11
    family relationships in, 51
    Instructions in, 75
    Numerical Progressions in, 83
    Organization of dots in, 3
    Orientation in Space I in, 19
    Orientation in Space II, 67
    problem solving in, 43
    Representational Stencil Design in, 107

    Syllogisms in, 99
    Temporal Relations in, 59
    Transitive Relations in, 91
Meaning, 118
Mediated Learning, ix
    ten criteria of, 118
Mental reconstruction, 109
Model building, 76
Multicultural activities
    Analytic Perception in, 30
    Categorization in, 38
    Comparisons in, 14
    family relationships in, 54
    Instructions in, 78
    Numerical Progressions in, 86
    Organization of Dots in, 6
    Orientation in Space I in, 22
    Orientation in Space II, 70
    problem solving in, 46
    Representational Stencil Design in, 111–112
    Syllogisms in, 102
    Temporal Relations in, 62
    Transitive Relations in, 94

Natural time, 57, 58
Nonverbal communication, 77
Novelty and challenge, 118
Numerical Progressions, 81–88
    application of, 82
    definition of, 82
    importance of, 82
    Representational Stencil design in, 116
    teaching in the community, 85–86
    teaching in the home, 84
    teaching in the schools, 83

Organization of Dots, 1–8
    applications of, 2
    definition of, 2
    importance of, 2
    Representational Stencil Design in, 115
    teaching in the community, 5–6
    teaching in the home, 4
    teaching in the school, 3
Orientation, definition of, 18
Orientation in Space I, 17–24
    applications of, 18, 66
    definition of, 18, 66
    importance of, 18, 66
    Representative Stencil Design and, 115
    teaching in schools, 19, 67
    teaching in the community, 21–22, 69–70
    teaching in the home, 20, 68
Output, 119
Overlapping sets theory, 101

Physical orientation, 18
Pictorial mode, 45
Play house, 76
Problem solving
    Analytic Perception in, 29
    application of, 42
    Comparisons in, 13
    cooperation as means of, 44
    definition of, 42
    importance of, 42
    Orientation in Space II in, 69
    teaching in the community, 45–46
    teaching in the home, 44
    teaching in the school, 43
Procrastination, 58
Proverbs in teaching Temporal Relations, 59
Psychological orientation, 18

Ranking skills, 91, 92, 93, 94
Reciprocity, 118
Relationships
    application of describing, 50
    definition of, 50
    teaching in the schools, 51
Representational Stencil Design, 105–116
    in Analytical Perception, 115
    application of, 106
    in categorization, 115
    in Comparisons, 115
    definition of, 106
    in Family Relations, 116
    in Illustrations, 115
    importance of, 106
    in Instructions, 116
    in Numerical Progressions, 116
    in Organization of Dots, 115
    in Orientation in sSpace I and II, 115
    in Syllogisms, 116
    teaching in the community, 109–111
    teaching in the home, 108
    teaching in the school, 107
    in Temporal Relations, 116
    in Transitive Relations, 116

School
    teaching Analytic Perception in, 27
    teaching Comparisons in, 11
    teaching Instructions in, 76
    teaching Numerical Progressions in, 84
    teaching Organization of Dots in, 3
    teaching Orientation in Space I in, 19
    teaching Orientation in Space II, 68
    teaching problem solving in, 43
    teaching Representational Stencil Design in, 108
    teaching Syllogisms in, 100
    teaching Temporal Relations in, 60
    teaching Transitive Relations in, 91
Self-change, 118
Self-regulation and control to behavior, 118
Sharing, 118
Shoe-house, 6
Space, definition of, 18
Study skills, 37
Syllogisms, 97–104
    application of, 98
    definition of, 98
    importance of, 98
    Representational Stencil Design in, 116
    teaching in the community, 101–102
    teaching in the home, 100
    teaching in the schools, 99
Synthesis, 25
    applications of, 26
    definition of, 26
    importance of, 26

Tangrams, 30
Temporal Relations, 57–64
    application of, 58
    definition of, 58
    importance of, 58
    Representational Stencil Design in, 116
    teaching in the community, 61–62
    teaching in the home, 60
    teaching in the school, 59
Time lines, in teaching Temporal Relations, 61
Time machines, 62
Timetables, in teaching Temporal Relations, 60
Transcendence, 118
Transitive Relations, 89–96
    applications of, 90
    definition of, 90
    importance of, 90
    Representational Stencil Design in, 116
    teaching in the community, 93–94
    teaching in the home, 92
    teaching in the school, 91
Tree house, 76
Twenty Questions game, 37

Venn diagrams in teaching Syllogisms, 99, 101
Vertical relationships, 53

Notes

Notes

Notes

Notes

ADDITIONAL
Instrumental Enrichment Resources

THE MAKING OF THE INDIVIDUAL
LEARNING HOW TO LEARN
An Interview with Reuven Feuerstein
Produced by James Bellanca
30-minute videotape $99.95....**#1224**
Feuerstein discusses how to prepare students for the twenty-first century by helping them learn how to learn, teaching with high expectations, and building thinking skills through mediated learning.

MAKING STUDENTS SMARTER
FROM THEORY TO PRACTICE
Reuven Feuerstein
Two 60-minute audio-
tapes $29.95....**#1227**
Psychologist Reuven Feuerstein, the creator of Instrumental Enrichment, discusses his theories of structural cognitive modifiability and mediated learning. Feuerstein believes all students, including the culturally disadvantaged, disabled, and underachieving gifted, can expand their intelligence. Learn the premise behind the theories and how they work.

ON FEUERSTEIN'S INSTRUMENTAL ENRICHMENT
A COLLECTION
Edited by Meir Ben-Hur
288 pages/paper $21.95....**#1256**
This collection offers readers a comprehensive look at the most recent writings about Instrumental Enrichment. The collection comprises three sections—the first explains Feuerstein's theory of cognitive modifiability, the second examines the latest research findings, and the third discusses the application of this methodology.

CHANGING CHILDREN'S MINDS
FEUERSTEIN'S REVOLUTION IN THE TEACHING OF INTELLIGENCE
Howard Sharron
381 pages/paper $32.00....**#1290**
This insightful book explores Feuerstein's theory that all children can learn. Learn how Instrumental Enrichment can empower underachieving students through the dynamic notion of intellectual potential.

THE MIND OF A CHILD
Videotape $40.00....**#1419**
A one-hour documentary that follows two extraordinary teachers and their work with aboriginal children in British Columbia and students in inner-city Washington, D.C. The film documents the breakthroughs these teachers experienced in adapting Reuven Feuerstein's theory of Instrumental Enrichment to their students.

WHAT IS IT ABOUT ME YOU CAN'T TEACH?
An Instructional Guide for the Urban Educator
Eleanor Reneé Rodriguez & James Bellanca
192 pages/paper $30.95....**#1444**
Beginning with Reuven Feuerstein's pioneering work, the authors of this valuable resource identify hundreds of practical classroom methods to help educators determine the best means for putting "high expectation" theory into practice in urban schools.

MEDIATED LEARNING IN AND OUT OF THE CLASSROOM
Manual Work Team of the Cognitive Research Program
208 pages/paper $30.95....**#1446**
This layperson's guide shows parents, teachers, and counselors how to implement professor Feuerstein's theory of mediated learning to enhance all children's learning potential. Mediated learning can improve students' impulse control, ability to make accurate comparisons, orientation in time and space, understanding of cause and effect, and other higher-order thinking processes.

TO ORDER THESE ITEMS, CALL
800-348-4474

2626 S. Clearbrook Dr., Arlington Heights, IL 60005
800-348-4474 • 847-290-6600 • (FAX) 847-290-6609

There are
one-story intellects,
two-story intellects, and
three-story intellects with skylights.

All fact collectors, who have no aim beyond their facts, are
one-story minds.

Two-story minds
compare, reason, generalize,
using the labors of the fact collectors
as well as their own.

Three-story minds
idealize, imagine, predict—their best illumination comes from above,
through the **skylight**.

—Oliver Wendell Holmes

SkyLight

PROFESSIONAL DEVELOPMENT

We Prepare Your Teachers Today for the Classrooms of Tomorrow

Learn from Our Books and from Our Authors!

Ignite Learning in Your School or District.

SkyLight's team of classroom-experienced consultants can help you foster systemic change for increased student achievement.

Professional development is a process not an event. SkyLight's experienced practitioners drive the creation of our on-site professional development programs, graduate courses, research-based publications, interactive video courses, teacher-friendly training materials, and online resources—call SkyLight Professional Development today.

SkyLight specializes in three professional development areas.

Specialty #1 — Best Practices

We **model** the best practices that result in improved student performance and guided applications.

Specialty #2 — Making the Innovations Last

We help set up **support** systems that make innovations part of everyday practice in the long-term systemic improvement of your school or district.

Specialty #3 — How to Assess the Results

We prepare your school leaders to encourage and **assess** teacher growth, **measure** student achievement, and **evaluate** program success.

Contact the SkyLight team and begin a process toward long-term results.

2626 S. Clearbrook Dr., Arlington Heights, IL 60005
800-348-4474 • 847-290-6600 • FAX 847-290-6609
info@skylightedu.com • www.skylightedu.com